The Invisible Customer

Strategies for Sucessful Customer Service
Down the Wire

Brian Clegg

**KOGAN
PAGE**

First published in 2000

Kogan Page Limited
120 Pentonville Road
London N1 9JN
UK

Kogan Page US
163 Central Avenue, Suite 2
Dover NH 03820
USA

British Library Cataloguing in Publication Data

A CIP record for this book is available from the British Library.

ISBN 0 7494 3144 X

Typeset by Kogan Page
Printed and bound in Great Britain by Clays Ltd, St Ives plc

Contents

Preface

Good customer service is an essential requirement to differentiate your company from the competition, yet new technology has opened a gap between customer expectations and service delivery. The inexorable move to call centres and Internet-based services is taking place alongside growing complaints about the lack of friendliness of these new customer interfaces.

Once upon a time all the technology jokes were about video recorders, but now touch-tone interactive voice response systems are on the receiving end of trouble-with-technology gags. Most people understand what it's like to spend half an hour punching through telephone menus until their index finger is numb, only to be told to ring a different number. The fact is that customer service through these vehicles is at best poor and at worst non-existent.

This is a field full of hardware and software vendors, trying to sell you the latest product to make your call centre work more effectively, or – with a typical use of acronyms – to link your ERP (Enterprise Resource Planning system) to your front office and BI (Business Intelligence) functionality to provide UBA (Universal Business Applications). The technology is important, and it does feature in this book, but in the end customer service is not about technology, but about people, and providing them with the products and services they are looking for in a way that they will appreciate.

You can make a difference, and this book can help. It is aimed at managers, and also at front-line call centre and Internet-based service staff. It may not be practical for everyone to attend a three-day customer-service course, but finding the time to read this book should help ensure that you, and your company, get a grip on giving the invisible customer great service. In this business, traditional timescales can be collapsed to a remarkable extent – and there may not be much time left

Acknowledgements

I would like to thank the many people and organizations that have provided me with information, interviews and case studies for this book, including: Roger Andrews, Art Technology Group, Paul Birch, Chris Brown, The Call Centre Association, John Carney, The Corel Corporation, Peter Cox, Nick Duffill, Dominic Ellis, Jessica Figueras, David Firth, Tony Flaherty, Nick Gassman, Rebecca Gunn, John Harris, Malcolm Harris, Dr Harish Kotadia, Adrian Lucas, Kylee Mackay, Brian Martin, John Matzen, Chip Maxwell, Ovum IT & Telecommunications Analysts, Oliver Picher, Keith Rapley, Unisys Corporation, Alice Venus, Bill Wittenberg and Joe Yaworski.

Thanks also to everyone at Kogan Page for getting this book together, but particularly to Pat Lomax for taking it on and Philip Mudd for proving that it's even possible to give great customer service (often remotely) to authors.

The invisible customer

This chapter introduces the world of the invisible customer. What is the point of good customer service? How does being remote from your customers make this particularly difficult? How will the book help?

No more face-to-face

There have never been more ways to deal with customers that you can't see. The traditional vehicle of the post is being overwhelmed by the tele-communications media – specifically the telephone and the Internet. The technological context makes it sound exciting, while from a business view-point there is the great benefit of reduced cost. Call centres are cheaper than high-street branches or stores. Web sites and e-mail are cheaper than call centres. All of a sudden it's possible to offer a 24-hour-a-day, seven-day-a-week service with fewer overheads than in a traditional operation with office hours.

But, and it's a big 'but', there is a danger that customer service will suffer. Before we go more into the practicalities of customer service for the invisible customer, it is important to establish that there's any point. Why should we bother about customer service?

Customer service matters

In the last 20 years we've rediscovered the value of customer service. As business guru Tom Peters points out in *The Circle of Innovation* (1998), practically any product or service from manufacturing to accountancy is in danger of becoming a commodity. There are too many competitors who are going to be just as good at getting the detail right and minimizing defects and all those other good things. If your business is going to stand out, though, the one thing that can consistently make a difference is great customer service.

At this point, someone usually mutters, 'But what about X?', where X is a company that does fantastically well despite a poor record on customer service. Often X is in the high-technology field, and its superb performance depends on turning out a stream of new and exciting products. This alone is a fragile basis for success. If you look at the Xs of the world they are often widely resented. Many customers will cheer when they go under.

Depending solely on your product is dangerous. Apart from anything else, you have to be incredibly nimble. Microsoft, the archetypal product-driven company, has demonstrated this. In not much more than a year, the giant corporation went from saying that the Internet was a non-commercial distraction to putting it at the centre of all its products. But as in so many things, Microsoft is the exception (for the moment). Whole product-driven industries have collapsed in the past when, faced with new developments, they have stuck their heads in the sand. Peters gives the example of the gas lighting industry at the start of the 20th century, which reacted to electricity by making a better gas lamp.

Just to stay in the game, you have to keep updating your product (or service), and on a regular basis you have to make it obsolete. But that alone isn't enough to make the grade. 'Ah,' someone may say, 'but what about companies that use superb marketing and strong brands to make their perfectly ordinary products a success? Can't they keep on top without worrying about customer service?' The label may give you an edge, but it's rarely enough in the long term. Relying on a label alone tempts your distribution channels to find ways of undercutting your margins, as many designer label companies are finding out when supermarkets sell grey imports at a fraction of the traditional designer price. I am not undervaluing the power of a good brand, but it can only take you so far. However good your product, however strong your brand, customer service is the only option to keep the gap between you and the opposition wide, and to keep your customers coming back time and time again.

Quick tips

Customer satisfaction rules

This is a view on the importance of customer satisfaction from a paper by Dr Harish Kotadia and Professor P T Srinivasan in the journal *Indian Management* (October 1997). Though originally referring to India, the lessons apply worldwide.

> Satisfied customers are the most profitable customers in any business and are the driving force behind sales and profit growth rates. They provide all the profits to a company and cover losses incurred by the business while dealing with other less-profitable customers. As satisfied customers determine profitability of a company, customer satisfaction is the best indicator of a company's future profits. The difference between a successful business and an unsuccessful one is the level of satisfaction of the customers.
>
> At a time when the financial performance of Indian companies is being challenged by increasing competition, fewer new customers and rising costs, the lifetime revenue generating potential of satisfied customers should not be underestimated and they should be treated as assets of the business. They are the guarantees to the business organization's future revenue inflows, reduced operating costs, higher margins and higher profitability.

Balance

It may be that by now you are shifting uncomfortably in your seat. 'What about cost savings?' you may ask. 'Of course we'd like to improve customer service, but it's not what the call centre or the Web site is here for. Our underlying aim is to deal with the customer as cheaply as possible.' We shall look at this in a bit more detail in the next section, but for now consider the possibility at least that savings alone aren't enough. If customer service is going to make a difference to your business survival, then you have to be prepared to pay for it. It's only reasonable to keep the costs required to a minimum, but seeing your remote customer function solely as a way of reducing costs, and hence having a 'get rid of the customer as quickly as possible' culture, is putting the cart before the horse.

Increasingly, call centres are taking a 'balanced scorecard' approach (see 'Measurement and monitoring', Chapter 16) to the measurement of success. This will involve conventional measures like waiting time and throughput, but will also consider the requirement to achieve customer satisfaction, and provide effective service.

What's it all for?

I'd like you to put aside any feelings you might have about missions and goals, and undertake the exercise outlined in the box below. Several of the other special sections in the book similarly include activities. Try to do them before you read further. If you don't, you will probably never get round to them and won't reap the benefits. Even if you never do such things normally, please try them – you can always throw the results away afterwards.

Action station

Where are we going?

Spend a few minutes thinking about the purposes of your remote customer service. Without going any further, take a sheet of paper and try to sum up in a single sentence what is at the heart of your operation. What is it all about? Don't take any notice of existing missions and goals, and whatever you do don't use 'missionese' (for example, 'to be the most excellent company in the sausage-making industry'). Make it from the heart, and specific.

Then list up to eight goals – specific things you want to achieve through your remote customer service operation. Don't worry if this is old hat to you, still do it, but base it on your own feelings, not company dogma.

Once you have done the exercise, look at what you have produced. Assess it in terms of likelihood of producing good customer service and likelihood of reducing cost. Look for areas where the two complement each other and areas where they are in conflict. How well does the reality match up to your goals? How well do your mission and goals match the twin needs for controlled costs and differentiation through excellent customer service? Do you need to bring in more elements from one side or the other to achieve a better balance?

Consider making a few bullet points for synergy and conflict, and keep them alongside as you read this book. If you find yourself thinking that a recommendation isn't going to save you money, check your lists and consider what you really want and need to be doing.

Good news story

Viking Direct

Viking Direct is a successful business stationery supplier. Traditionally their business comes in by telephone, fax and mail, but an interactive Web site is proving increasingly popular with customers. This is a good example of a balanced win that is providing benefits for the company and the customer simultaneously.

For the company there is cost saving. The site is less costly per transaction than a telephone call, and is less likely to involve costly errors than a fax order. For the customer, there is the potential for cost saving too as, like many companies, Viking offers financial incentives for shopping this way. There are further benefits. Orders can be placed whenever the customer wants. Goods can be selected in more flexible ways, for example, by browsing online as through a catalogue, or entering the order code direct from a paper catalogue, which becomes beneficial when dealing with a supplier that sends out a large number of catalogues with varying sale offers. Finally, for the customer, the order is constantly totalled, so that there is no effort in assessing what has been spent or the effect of, for instance, doubling a particular stock item. It is not always possible, but win–win is a practical outcome for many transactions with the invisible customer.

Achieving a balance in such circumstances is not trivial. One powerful tool that may help is the balanced scorecard (see Chapter 16 for more details).

We've been doing it for years

Why is so much emphasis being put on customer service? Everyone has been providing it for years, haven't they? Sadly, they haven't. Customer service is still mediocre in many companies. The best stand out far above the rest.

It is worth spending a little while thinking about the realities. Take the ordinary, day-to-day experiences you have in the high street. You go into a fast-food restaurant, once held up as the epitome of good customer service, but there aren't quite enough staff, so queues have built up. The server uses all the magic words, but is obviously reciting them by rote – her face doesn't echo the welcome of her script. The food, when it arrives, is hot and matches specification, but the server doesn't bother to put any napkins in the bag, and doesn't ask if you'd like any dips. The delivery just isn't there. You go into another store and ask for something that isn't on the shelf. The sales assistant says, 'I suppose I could look in the stockroom for you.' He obviously doesn't want to. You make a joke about it, and he stares at you blankly.

Conventional shops have got much better at the mechanics of customer service, for example with queuing systems and scripts, and by getting their staff to appear friendly and helpful, but very few go far enough.

Good news story

Disney Stores

This example isn't specific to handling the invisible customer, but emphasizes the difference that real customer service makes. Walk into the Disney Store in Edinburgh, and you will see how to do customer service well. You are greeted pleasantly on your way in. As you browse, you are asked if you need help, especially if you are looking at the clothes. The sales assistant (sorry, cast member) really seems to want to help. When you get to the till, she exchanges easy conversation that obviously isn't following a script. When she points out a special offer of a free picture if you pre-order a video, she immediately agrees with your observation that, with two children, such a gift is more of a problem than a bonus. On the bill you are referred to as a guest.

The Disney cast member/guest role concept is familiar, but needs care and effort to make it work. What makes the experience superb? Assistance is always available, but not too pushy. You feel you are having a conversation with an intelligent person who isn't working to a script. The cast member seems geninely interested in you and what you are trying to buy. For Disney the word 'guest' isn't an empty label; you are really treated that way. Yet this is achieved in a country with a totally different national character to the United States without feeling like cultural imperialism. When we're considering customer service online and on the phone, we should be aiming for just as much distinction as Disney manages to put in a typical store.

Customer, what customer?

Customer service is a big deal everywhere, but the central theme of this book, the invisible customer, adds an extra complexity to the need. We are moving into an age when more and more of our customers never see us, and we never see them. The call centre and the Internet are changing the face of customer contact, or rather lack of contact. It seems as though hardly a day passes without the announcement of job losses as a result of increasing use of telephone services or Internet sales.

Such a move throws up many problems. If we can't see our customers, there is an inclination to treat them more casually than we would face to face. As is described in later chapters, it's all too easy to put people at the end of phone lines or sitting at computers through the kind of unpleasant experience that would be unthinkable if they were in front of us. We make them wait, effectively ignoring them. We make them perform irritating tasks, selecting from interminable menus, only to discover that 'all of our agents are busy right now'. We are off-hand with them. We make them wait for days to get a response to an e-mail query; quite often we never respond at all.

Action station

Be a customer

If your business model makes it possible, get through to your call centre or connect to your Web site as a customer. How easy is it to find your way around? Before getting in touch, think of a complex question to ask, the sort of thing that is unlikely to be handled by an agent on the spot, or by online help. How long does it take to get a reply in such circumstances, and how do you get it? How did the overall experience make you feel? You aren't going to do anything more with this right now. It may be that you thought everything was just fine. Excellent. But equally, the outside-in experience might not have been too great. Of course you know lots of reasons why it had to be the way it was, but the ordinary customers don't. And that's what matters.

If you've got this far and didn't try out the activity, go back and do it. If you work in a call centre or online service centre, rather than managing one, you aren't let off this exercise. There's a feeling that 'This is nothing to do with me, it's management's problem', but getting customer service right is in everyone's interest. It's not just a matter of keeping your job, though that might be a consideration. It's also about making more of your job and your life. If you are providing the service, you ought to know what it's like to receive it. Go back and give the exercise a try now.

Sites and agents

As this book will be constantly referring to both Web sites and call centres, I've used the term 'site' to mean either. Similarly, I have used the term 'agents' throughout to signify both call centre staff and those who provide Internet or e-mail support. The distinction is often vague anyway, as it is not unusual for call centres to provide the company's Internet support.

Where do we go from here?

Given the need for customer service and the difficulties of providing good customer service from a site, what can be done about it? The rest of the book gives the answers. We will begin by looking at the experience from the point of view of the customer. From there we move on through two bridging chapters (Chapters 8 and 9) to come to the requirements of the site, before pulling it all together into an agenda for action.

Table 1.1 Questions explored in this book

Chapter	Questions
Chapter 2: Getting through	What's it like getting through to your site? How can you make it easier?
Chapter 3: The first contact	What is the first contact the customer has with you like? How can you make it better?
Chapter 4: Exploration	Are there ways customers can help themselves? How can you make it easier and quicker to get to the right part of your site? How can you give customers the choice of helping themselves as much as possible?
Chapter 5: A cry for help	Is it possible for customers to get help on using the site? Is it possible to get help on your products and services from the site? How can you make each type of help easier to obtain and more relevant?
Chapter 6: Getting the glow	Is it possible to make using your site a pleasant experience? How can you give customers that glow? Can you cope with difficult customers and still make them feel they had good customer service?
Chapter 7: Long-distance selling	Can your customers buy the products and services they want from your site? Is it easy for them to find the right product for their needs? How flexible is the sales mechanism? How much support do you give to the buying process? Is it possible to make cold calls pleasant for the recipient?

Table 1.1 continued

Chapter 8: Speed and content	Is the whole experience of dealing with your site quick enough? Does your site have the right content? Do you deliver on your promises?
Chapter 9: Who are those customers?	Is it possible to really know your customers from a distance? Are there advantages for the customers in being known? Are there advantages for you in knowing the customers? What mechanisms can help with knowing customers?
Chapter 10: You can't get the staff	Why is staff retention poor in call centres? How can you get the right sort of people to be agents? How can you keep the right sort of people? Does having the right sort of people make a difference?
Chapter 11: Training and learning	What types of training will help agents? What ongoing learning will improve customer service?
Chapter 12: Roles and empowerment	Why is it important that agents buy into the company's objectives? How can the agent's role be modified to improve buy-in? What can be done to give the agent the ability to get things done?
Chapter 13: Process rules	What processes do your customers use? How should your approach match customer processes? How can you take a process-oriented approach without becoming inflexible?

Table 1.1 continued

Chapter 14: Stressed out	Why is stress important to agents and to the company? What makes working in a site stressful? How can stress be managed?
Chapter 15: Technology triumphs	What can technology do to help? Is technology enough on its own? How does technology get in the way of good customer service?
Chapter 16: Driven change	Once things have been improved, is there any need to do more? What difference can the competition make? What difference does technology make? How can changing customer expectations change requirements? How do you keep on top of change?
Chapter 17: The invisible agenda	Where do you start? What should you be doing as individuals? What should you be doing as a company?

So we begin our exploration from the viewpoint of the customer. The customer has found out about us. It may be through advertising, or a directory, or personal recommendation – it doesn't really matter how at this stage. He or she wants to contact us. (We'll look at cold calls in Chapter 7, 'Long-distance selling'.) Why then do we make it so difficult? Let's look at the good news and the bad news about getting through.

2

Getting through

Being found by the customer isn't the focus of this book, but establishing contact is still the starting point of the customer relationship. Getting an engaged tone or being put straight on hold is not a good start to that relationship. This chapter looks at when to answer the phone; the benefits of having a Web site or e-mail address that can be guessed; the dangers of slavishly following design trends; and the importance of keeping up with e-mail developments.

Here we are!

We aren't hugely concerned in this book with making your site visible – the assumption is that the customer already knows how to make contact – but it is, of course, an issue. How you make your means of contact available to the customer is crucial. For example, television advertising may be good to increase customer awareness of your availability, but few people sit by the TV with pen and paper ready, just in case a useful number flashes up half-way through their favourite soap opera. They are more likely to register your existence, then look you up at a later date in the Yellow Pages or some other contact directory. If you are providing telephone support for an existing product, that number should be readily available to the consumer, and not just in a service booklet that they throw away. Thinking through the vehicles for getting your contact details across is an essential.

With Internet access, the challenge is even greater. Entering your addresses in search engines is an obvious requirement, but not the only one. Making sure that your Web address is emblazoned on all your products and packaging is another step, while getting as much possible coverage in the media is equally valuable.

You should make it easy for customers who want to deal with you to locate your Web site. If they are browsing through a paper catalogue, the Web site should be emblazoned across each page, enticing them to your location. If they look you up in the Yellow Pages phone book, your Web address should be just as visible as your phone number. If they see an advertisement in a magazine or newspaper, the Web site should leap out. A Web contact is the cheapest customer service you can manage – why make it difficult for the customer?

Action station

Finding yourself

Spend half an hour pretending to be a customer. Using the typical tools – Web search engines, newspapers, Teletext, phone book, Yellow Pages – see just how easy it is to locate your site, and how much you know about the advantages of using it before you get there.

Many companies offer some benefit to the customer for using the Web site. Perhaps delivery is free, or there are extra bells and whistles on the product for no extra charge, or there's a discount over other means of contact. Online bank Egg even offers extra interest on its accounts for customers who stick to online access. The existence of such advantages should be broadcast alongside the Web address. Many companies don't tell customers why it's to their advantage to use the Web site, and then, when few use it, conclude that the Web isn't a good way to interact with customers.

It is worth remembering what the medium is called: the World Wide Web. Note particularly the 'Web' bit. It is called a web because there are millions of links crossing from page to page and site to site across the world. These links are often the mechanism a newcomer will use to get to your site. It is worth putting a little effort into ensuring that your site has links from other appropriate sites. Consider all the possible places your customers might come from:

- Portal sites – search engines and the 'home' sites of Internet Service Providers. Do you have a personal presence there?
- Special interest sites – whatever your business, there will probably be commercial sites that cover it. Are there links from them?
- Personal sites – somewhere out on the Web someone is interested in what you do. They will have set up a personal site, which will attract others with similar interests. If you can get them to link to your site (and they will usually be flattered to be asked), you have found a new route in for your customers.

If you aren't sure where to look for these sites, check out Internet Service Providers in a catalogue like Yahoo. To find special interest and personal sites, put the keywords that best describe your business into a number of search engines. Plough through as many sites as you can, looking for potentially appealing sites that might reap customers for you. If your customers aren't entirely US-based, look in other countries' search engines too.

To charge or not to charge

The toll-free number has become a commodity for much of business. You don't gain any real advantage over the competition by having it, but you will certainly feel a disadvantage if you haven't got it. Against this background, there are still a number of business models where it is felt that a toll free number doesn't make business sense. Before you scrap charging and go toll free, or before you abandon your free call facility, consider the balance involved.

If you are advertising a service in a directory like Yellow Pages, toll free is a near necessity. There is a distinction between advertising and being listed. If your only purpose in appearing in Yellow Pages is that someone who knows your name can find your number, it is not necessary to go toll free. If, however, you want to catch the passing trade that is looking for a particular kind of vendor in the directory, you need to use a combination of a display advertisement and a toll free number.

Where companies have been more inclined to move away from toll free is in customer support. Some companies have even moved to using premium rate lines for their customer support lines. Classic examples of this approach are the 'free' Internet Service Providers who don't charge for connection to the Internet, and software vendors. The 'free' ISPs are in an interesting position. They get their revenue from a combination of a cut of the telephone call charge, and sales and advertising from their portal site. Such companies often charge premium rates for support. Similarly software companies are increasingly charging for support, finding that the support costs of their software rises and rises as computers get more complex and the market spreads worldwide.

It is a close call whether or not they have made the appropriate decision for their business. In markets where one product leads the others by a long way it would seem an acceptable strategy. Few customers will opt for a non-standard approach just to avoid paying for a phone call. Where, however, there is relatively little to distinguish your service from the others, providing free telephone support is a very sensible competitive move. This is especially true in markets that involve high-technology sales to non-technical people, who are likely to need the support more and would rather pay a little extra up front to insure against big phone bills when everything goes to pieces.

The engaged tone

Not getting through at all is the ultimate nightmare for remote customer service. As soon as the customer gets the engaged tone, or the Web browser says that there's no such address, you have a major problem. What measures do you have in place to check that this isn't happening? Regard the engaged tone or the disappeared address as a major evil. You might think that you've only lost a few customers, but remember what those customers represent. They all have a lifetime value to your company, the amount they would spend with you if they remained customers for the rest of their lives. This can be a huge amount.

Horror story

The missing nuts

A major international airline was going through one of the regular cost-cutting exercises that all airlines (and most corporates) regularly engage in. An accountant had worked out that the company could save $10,000 a year, just by stopping providing little packets of nuts with the drinks in the first-class cabin.

Within days of implementing the change, the complaints began to pile in. One customer, who threatened never to fly with the airline again, pointed out that he crossed the Atlantic Ocean with them at least twice a week. In round figures, this customer alone was worth around $30,000 a year. If he carried on for 20 years, that was a total of $600,000 lost from one customer to save peanuts. The nuts were reinstated immediately.

There are two lessons to be learnt from this story. The first is the importance of taking lifetime value into account: losing a regular customer for ever is an expensive business. The second is the impact that apparently trivial aspects of service can have. Before you dismiss the value to the customer of your toll free number, or of putting money and effort into customer service, remember the peanuts. In the end transatlantic flights are much of a muchness – a small detail like nuts can be enough to push a customer elsewhere. The lesson applies equally well to the service from your call centre or Web site.

To make matters worse, your disgruntled customers are more likely to spread news about a failure than happy customers are about a good experience. It's not that they won't tell their friends if you do something outstanding – but it has to be outstanding and not just good. If they can't get through to you, not only will you lose their custom, but they will go around saying, 'Don't bother ringing Mycorp – all you ever get is an engaged tone.'

How long to wait

So the phone is ringing, or the browser claims to have found the site. How long will it be before something happens? With the Web site, it has to be as fast as possible. Look at your server throughput capacities, how and where they are connected to the Internet, and all the usual considerations for Web performance. Ask the designer if there is some way to get your home page displayed faster. See if it is possible to get a usable skeleton of the page in place while still waiting for the slower graphics to load. If your customer base is worldwide, consider having local sites that can provide faster response times for your distributed customers. This all costs money, but there is good evidence that Web customers are the least patient on the planet. The ease with which they can browse off to an alternative site means that they may well zip elsewhere if they aren't up and running with your site in under 10 seconds. Resist the urge to throw in all the graphics from your corporate report and accounts. Doubly resist the urge to allow a traditional graphics designer who is unfamiliar with the size/speed equation of the Web loose on your site. We'll consider this further, later in the chapter.

On the phone, waiting is a more complex issue. An absolutely immediate answer can be off-putting. Customers need a couple of seconds to get their thoughts in order. Two or three rings is generally considered most acceptable. However, long periods of ringing can be almost as bad as getting an engaged tone. Anything over around 20 seconds gives the impression that either you don't care or you aren't even there. Expect to lose a lot of customer brownie points (and customers) if this happens.

Instant on hold

What happens after the phone is answered is considered in the next chapter, but it is appropriate to mention one possible response here, which is effectively to answer the phone yet not answer at the same time. When callers are immediately put on hold, they may have the assurance that the company is still there, but they are still waiting – what's more, at their own expense. As with any caller holding on, around 20 seconds ought to be the maximum. At the very least give them the chance of leaving a message and giving up. Don't think, by the way, that you can fool people into thinking that they aren't paying to be on hold by starting up an internal ringing tone immediately after they get through. Many callers can spot this happening.

Guess the site and the e-mail

The Internet has one huge advantage over the telephone. It does not use obscure numbers to connect you to it. (Actually, it does use numbers, but there is a naming system that lets you type in a more readable address, which is then automatically transformed into numbers.)

Action station

The memory game

Next time you are watching TV (or listening to the radio), look out for a show that provides contact details. Try to remember the telephone number and e-mail address without writing them down. Ten minutes later, see what you can remember.

The chances are that the telephone number will have gone straight out of your mind. It's not surprising. Your short-term memory can only cope with seven or eight digits at once, so remembering a telephone number requires complex mental juggling to keep it in mind. But it's equally difficult to force the number into longer-term memory, because it lacks imagery and associations – the stuff that memories are made of. Chances are, the number will disappear very quickly. Words, on the other hand, have lots of associations that make it easy to tie them straight into longer-term memory. An e-mail address, if properly designed, will stick with you.

As the exercise above shows, provided you design your e-mail address or Web site address correctly, it is likely to be very easy to remember. In fact, an Internet-savvy person could well guess it. It is worth making sure that any address the public is likely to use is easy to guess. This is both to help people to guess it from scratch, and to make it easier to remember.

Web sites should stick to the common formats. Make sure that your site will accept the address with or without the 'www' at the start. Use the.com (or.co.uk, or whichever country is involved) format rather than more obscure ones. Don't put dots or underscores in the company name. Similarly, try to avoid contractions that aren't well known. It's sensible for Cable Network News to use CNN for its Web site. It is less sensible for a company called The Big Company to use www.bigco.com unless BigCo is a common nickname.

Whatever address you choose, you can't guarantee to match the customer's guess. Web technology can help here. It is technically easy to map a number of addresses on to the same site. So whether customers type thebigcompany.com or tbc.com or bigco.com, they should be able to get to you.

I recently had a good example of difficulty in guessing a Web site, when trying to find the site of that remarkable store, Liberty. After some searching it turned out that the address was www.liberty-plc.co.uk – almost impossible to guess. Not only is there a hyphen in the name, but the 'plc' bit makes it an unlikely choice. It would have been much better to have gone for both.com and.co.uk endings, and variants on its best known name such as www.libertyoflondon.co.uk and www.libertysoflondon.co.uk. What about the most obvious address of all – www.liberty.co.uk? In fact it was the first one I tried, but turned out to belong to an image capture and data management company. Domain names, the technical term for the location part of an Internet address, are assigned on a first-come, first-served basis, provided there is no evidence that the company wants the address in order to blackmail another potential owner. Liberty can't just storm in and take over www.liberty.co.uk. However, there is nothing to stop it approaching Liberty the data management company and asking if it could have a link from the front page. This might involve a small fee, but would be worth it if just one paying customer made the transition to its site. In other cases – the Web search engine AltaVista is a good example – it has proved worth buying the most obvious domain name from its current owner.

Similar consideration should be given to e-mail addresses. If possible, provide an address which has function before the @ sign and company after, for example support@xyz.com. Where you are giving an individual's e-mail address (and this is highly recommended once a relationship is established), you will be restricted by the naming convention adopted by your company. However, if you are at a stage where it is possible to influence the naming convention, there are a number of ways you can make it more friendly. It is preferable not to use dots to separate names (eg, fred.bloggs@mycorp.com), as it is an Internet convention not to use dots at the left of the @ sign. Don't use hyphens or underscores either, but run the names together. I would recommend using a full first name, rather than an initial. Go for fredbloggs@mycorp.com or fredb@mycorp.com rather than fbloggs@mycorp.com. This looks more accessible to the customer. If you think that the fredb format is too small-company for you, that's what Microsoft uses. If your customers are unfamiliar with the convention of showing e-mail addresses all in lower case, you might like to use appropriate capitals, eg FredBloggs@ Mycorp.com. Unlike file names on the Internet, addresses are not case-sensitive, so there is no difference between FredBloggs and fredbloggs.

What's in a number?

While phone numbers will never have the memorability of Web addresses, some things can be done to improve their customer friendliness. The use of letters on the telephone keypad has always been popular in the US ('call 800-THISNUM') and is having something of a resurgence in the UK. Repeated number patterns can also be valuable. But the most important thing is having a simple contact scheme.

Horror story

Hunt BT

This customer found a company in chaos, although it is one that should know better than most how to make its contact scheme work.

BT, the UK's largest telecommunications provider and now a worldwide corporation, has a scheme where customers can nominate a set of numbers as 'key numbers', which receive a discount on each call. When I got my business bill I found that these key numbers, which should have applied to all three of my business numbers, weren't correctly set up.

The telephone bill shows four numbers to call for help, for bill enquiries, sales, fault reporting and customer service respectively. I tried the customer service number. After pressing a few buttons on a voice system I spoke to a real person, who said I should ring the key numbers hotline. The hotline said that they could enter new numbers, but to link my lines I needed to call 152, BT's generic business service number. The agent on 152 gave me yet another freephone number to ring. I was rather baffled when the message started 'Welcome to Orange' (one of BT's competitor telephone companies).

I went back to 152. Now came the most hilarious bit. I pointed out that the number they had given me put me through to Orange. The agent said, 'Yes, it's strange. I think it's done that for me too.' 'What, to put in my BT key numbers I need to speak to Orange?' 'Just a minute, I'll check.' She came back and told me I needed to speak to the key numbers hotline. 'But they were the ones who put me on to 152.' She was so sure that she put me through directly to the hotline. When I'd explained, they told me that I would need to speak to sales. Finally, I found someone who could help, only to tell me that the call in which I'd changed all my key numbers a week before had been ignored. Finally, to add insult to injury, they had to ask my address to send me a confirmation letter.

It's not the cost of the calls – they were all freephone numbers – but the time taken. Each time I had to dial a different number. Each time I had to give my name, my business name and my phone number. It took a total of seven calls to get a simple transaction made. It's not good enough.

This customer discovered just how badly things can go wrong without a simple handling system. When the company giving the customer service is the telephone company, they have a real potential advantage. They can use special, easy-to-remember, short numbers like 152. Why BT has decided then to confuse the issue by using a plethora of other numbers (one of them apparently belonging to Orange) is beyond comprehension. How much better it would have been for the customer if she had only had to ring 152, and be put through to the appropriate place.

The only possible argument for having different incoming numbers is to help sort out the purpose of the call – yet at least one of the BT lines had a 'receptionist' who directed the call to the right person, and two others had interactive voice response (IVR) systems doing this filtering. A single number would have been much better for everyone. It is to be hoped that this wonderful example of how not to do it will help other companies get it right.

Instant Web site?

Getting through quickly is not an issue only on the phone. Just because you have a Web site doesn't mean that your customers will get through quickly. The problem is made complex by the multiple layers of connection that get in the way of a link to a Web site. The customer is sitting on top of a whole multi-decker pyramid of possible causes of delay.

The jam-up starts with the physical connection between the customer and the ISP, which can be anything from a modem running at 9,600 bits per second to ADSL at 6,000,000 bits per second. A customer with a low-end modem can have problems trying to use a site that makes a lot of use of graphics. For example, a small picture might be 10 kilobytes in size, which is 80,000 bits, and will take about six seconds to get on to your customer's screen. You might think that six seconds isn't a long time, but think of an interaction with a Web site as a conversation. A six-second delay would become infuriating if you were talking to someone.

There are plenty of other potential delays in the system. Many customers still use analogue connections (modems) rather than digital (ISDN and above). They are particularly susceptible to poor-quality lines and data loss, which slow down the transmission. Typically, the customer will pass through an Internet Service Provider. A popular, or an under-resourced, ISP can provide its own bottleneck. The connection then has to pass through the various circuits that will get it your server. The possible failings are still not over. Your server may not be fast enough, or could be suffering from a sudden unusual load.

Finally, there's the nature of the Internet itself. In return for flexibility of routing and offering capacity to a huge number of potential users, the

Internet uses a protocol for communication that is inherently likely to intro-duce some delays. By splitting your communication up into small packets you get lots of flexibility, but the packaging itself takes up bandwidth, and packets can collide or get lost, requiring the system to ask for a new one, all adding to potential delays.

With all these possible barriers to quick access to your site, you need to make sure that, as a company, you are breaking through as many as possi-ble. You might not see yourself as responsible for users' modems or their ISPs, but if customers are held up, it's still a problem for you. You might be able to help by pointing them to more appropriate connections. You will certainly be able to help them by having lots of bandwidth into a very fast server, and a Web site where the pages don't take long to load. Whatever steps you take, be aware of the problem.

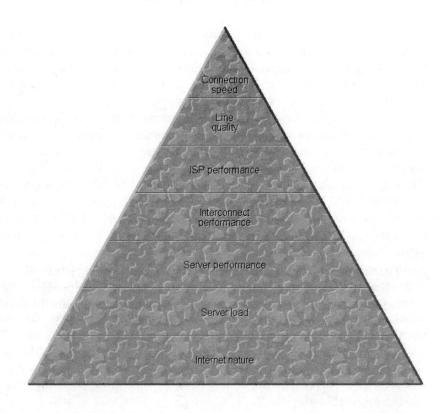

Figure 2.1 Internet bottlenecks

Designer nightmare

The appearance of your Web site results from the dynamic tension between two requirements – usability and style. It might seem obvious that a well-designed site should also be easy to use, but there are few environments more strongly driven by style than the Web. It's not that style is a bad thing – far from it – but the evidence is that when style becomes the prime criterion, practicality goes out of the window.

As Donald Norman points out in his brilliant book *The Psychology of Everyday Things* (1988), there is a class of things that we should be able to use effortlessly in an everyday way, which we find difficult to use in practice. Norman humorously suggests that such products 'must have won a prize': there's no other explanation for their obscure pursuit of design over usability. There's a battle under way between a product that looks good to the eye and one that fulfils its role with simple ease.

Take just a couple of the examples Norman gives. There is hardly anything simpler than a door. Designers love clean, unbroken lines, so they will often produce a line of glass doors in shopping malls, so beautifully crafted that you can't see the hinges, and so exquisitely simple that there is no handle. Result? A whole stream of frustrated people. They try to get in through the plain glass panels between the doors. They try to push on the hinge side of the door instead of the opening side. Eventually someone sticks an ugly 'push here' label on the door, spoiling the whole effect.

Another example of designer door madness can be seen at British Airways' superb-looking Waterside headquarters building. Designers love symmetry and plain lines. Because of this, they like to put the same door furniture on both sides of the door. The result on the entrances to the washrooms at Waterside is that each door has a long, stylish pull handle – which you have to push. This way there's the same handle on both sides of the door, and a whole stream of people pulling the door against the stop, looking foolish and then pushing it, and inclined to blame themselves for getting it wrong.

Consider also the humble domestic stove, a simple enough product. Why is it that every time I use my cooker, despite owning it for 10 years, I have to peer at the label to see which knob controls which burner? It's because the knobs are all in a row, although the burners are laid out in a square. As Norman points out, if the knobs were in a layout that roughly matched the hob, there would be no need for labels, as it would be obvious which knob to use.

What are the lessons for a Web site? You should make it look good, but don't let the style get in the way of making it easy to use. Consider all kinds of user. Will they all be able to find their way around without help, or will some be overwhelmed? Bear in mind that there are broadly two types of user. Some will just be surfing around, and you should feel free to go over the top entertaining them. Others will want to come to your site to get something done as quickly as possible and get out again. Help them to achieve their goals.

Quick tips

Top ten don'ts for Web site design

1. Don't use big images in your main site. Point to where users can open big images, if appropriate. If a page won't load in a few seconds on a typical connection, you are going to lose custom.
2. Don't depend on all the latest hi-tech add-ins. Make sure your site is viewable on any reasonable browser. You might also consider avoiding the commonly used frames feature for this reason – some of the most popular Web sites do.
3. Don't hide functionality. Ever since the Apple Mac, we have been using menus and toolbars to make the functionality of a program visible. Don't reverse the trend.
4. Don't change site design too often. Regular customers like familiarity. Redesign often enough to keep your style current, but don't put the customers off.
5. Don't make the site impenetrable. Some designs use such clever navigation techniques that you can't bookmark a page and come back to it – you always come back to the home page. This will put people off returning.
6. Don't forget text-only. Text-only sites are valuable for those using special hardware (Web phones, personal organizers, etc), those with very low connection speeds, and blind customers. Make sure you have a readily available text-only site.
7. Don't let art overwhelm legibility. If your artwork is designed for maximum impact, you may find it makes it impossible to read the text. If customers can't read it, they won't buy.
8. Don't have too much movement. Animation on Web sites can now be quite sophisticated, but too much animation results in confusion for customers.
9. Don't hog the browser. Some Web sites using frames keep control of the browser even if the customer follows a link away from your site. This might seem superficially attractive as you remain 'in control', but the result is often that the other Web site is messed up and the customer is irritated. Similarly, don't put linked pages into mini-windows with no controls.
10. Don't take your designer's word for it that the site is usable. He or she is much too biased. Get an external view.

The last tip in the box above is one of the most important. A specific example is that of hyperlinks (the bits of text you can click on to move elsewhere). Traditionally, they have been underlined. This makes them stand out very clearly, but they also look clumsy, as it isn't usual to have underlined words in printed text. A fair number of the more sophisticated Web sites have links that aren't underlined. They use different colours, or they change appearance when you run a cursor over them. That's fine if you aren't colour-blind, the contrasts work well on your particular screen and you bother to trawl the surface of the document looking for links. Arguably, despite the importance of good looks, visibility of links is more important in hypertext.

Handling e-mail formats

A problem that is sometimes faced, especially by large companies, is difficulty in handling different e-mail formats. If the company's own e-mail system isn't Internet-based, it may struggle with certain aspects of e-mail. It used to be the case that attachments (documents and other computer files accompanying an e-mail) weren't always well handled. This has mostly been sorted out, but a more insidious problem is dealing with HTML mail.

Traditional e-mail was straightforward text without anything to indicate layout, or different fonts and weights of typeface. The new standard, HTML mail, uses the same mechanisms as the Web to give e-mail a richer, more interesting appearance. Most modern mail programs can handle HTML mail, but you may find that the gateway that links your company's systems to the Internet gets confused and either loses the HTML or strips it off into an attachment, so you end up with a much more confusing mail than the original one sent. If you are serious about doing customer service by e-mail, it should be a priority to ensure that your mail systems can cope with HTML mail. It is technically possible; don't believe vendors who tell you otherwise.

You ought to bear the reverse in mind too. If your customers' mail systems don't support HTML, you don't want to be forcing fancy formatting on them that they can't cope with. The ideal approach is to respond in the same format that you receive. If you don't know what the customer can cope with, use plain text, but have an option to switch up easily to the HTML version.

What happens next

So, one way or another, your customer has got through to you. What happens next in those first few crucial seconds can make or break your customer service quality. We are on to the point of first contact.

3

The first contact

The customer has found you and initiates a contact. It's a cliché that the first few seconds are crucially important, but it's true nevertheless. This chapter looks at just what invisible customers will come across on their first contact with you, and how to make those first steps as pleasant as possible.

A warm welcome

I recently rang up Standard Life Bank, one of the UK's rapidly growing telephone banks. Not only did they score on responsiveness by answering within two rings, but I felt a warm glow of pleasure – because a real person asked me what I wanted. It's interesting that an element of my good feelings about this call came from the expectation that I was going to face an automated device with a series of menus to struggle through and further waits in store. It doesn't matter how often you tell customers that an automated voice system is 'for your convenience', they won't be convinced. They know that it is there to save the company money, so don't try to fool them. This view is shared by Standard Life's MD, Jim Spowart. Standard Life handles some 3,000 calls per day in two call centres, but the company has intentionally avoided obtrusive technology in its call centres, and interactive voice response (IVR) in particular. Mr Spowart is adamant that a customer should *always* be put straight through to an operator.

From a customer service viewpoint, making a human being the first point of contact in a general telephone service is highly desirable. There are circumstances when an IVR system will provide customer service benefits, but bear in mind the customer service component. A parallel is the use of through-the-wall automated teller machines (ATMs) at banks. These have been a major success, to the extent that it is quite common to see a queue at a machine while a human bank clerk sits without customers. However, things might have been quite different if ATMs had been introduced in the same way that IVR tends to be, that is, if a traditional bank branch had simply been replaced by a bunch of ATMs. Instead, customer service has been built in because the ATMs are usually either an optional extra to the human teller – the customer has the choice which to use – or because ATMs have been used to reach environments like supermarkets where cash was not previously available.

Transferring the ATM model into the voice response world would give voice response a whole new press, for example, by having voice response as a possible option rather than the only option. This could be approached by having separate, clearly identified numbers for a human point of contact or voice response. It is also possible to give the option of voice response while waiting for a human operator. At first sight this is not very different from the traditional voice menu that gives an option at the end to wait for an operator if you do nothing. However, there is a big psychological difference. With the traditional menu, dealing with a person is the last resort. With the alternative, you will be dealing with a person, but while you wait you can divert to a voice menu – miles apart in feel.

The negative impact of voice response can be reduced by making it a means of providing service where none would otherwise be available. If, for example, your normal services are only available during office hours, having a voice system to handle customers out of hours will give a better level of service than simply telling them to come back later.

Frankenstein's telephonist

To say that IVR has a bad press is a bit like saying Vlad the Impaler was not a nice man. IVR has replaced video recorder programming as the chief butt of anti-technology jokes. Take this suggestion of how IVR might be employed by the fire service, told by Malcolm Harris of the call centre support company, Call Centre Selection:

Thank you for calling the Fire Department. If your school class would like to visit a fire station, please press 1. If you would like to sit in a fire truck and hear the siren, press 2. If you would like to turn yourself in for a recent arson, press 3. If you are a fireman and would like to know what shift you are on this week, press 4. If you recently had a fire and it has started up again, press 5. If you would like to report a new fire, press 6.

If you are calling from a business, press 1. If you are at a government agency, press 2. If you are at an amusement park, press 3. If you are in a vehicle, press 4. If you are at a residence, press 5.

If you smell something funny and/or can see smoke and just think there may be a fire, press 1. If you dropped a burning cigarette and cannot find it, press 2. If your car is on fire, press 3. If you are on fire, press 4. If you can actually see the fire, press 5.

Thank you for reporting a fire. Please enter your five-digit zip code... long pause... You have entered SEVEN-FIVE-TWO-FOUR-FOUR. If this is correct, press 1.

One moment while we open a new case file for you...

If you have called the fire department within the last 30 days, press 1. If you have called the fire department before, but it was not an emergency, press 2. If you have called the fire department before and it was an emergency, press 3. If this is the first time you have called the fire department, press 4.

It is at this moment that you notice that the phone has gone dead, because the phone cord has melted...

It's funny because it is all too close to the truth, and because it illustrates neatly the fact that IVR is not there to benefit customers, however much you say it. What it also shows is how not to build an IVR script. We'll come back to this and some of the lessons that can be learnt in the section 'The nature of the beast' (see below).

If IVR is so awful, should it be used at all? Jim Spowart of Standard Life Bank has proved that IVR cannot be regarded as a business imperative. However, there are circumstances where it can give benefit. We've already seen the ATM model, providing a picture of IVR systems that give a total service without reference to human beings. These have a real benefit out of hours and for very simple transactions like a bank-balance enquiry. There is also a benefit for the customer where a very shallow IVR tree is used to direct a call to the right person. If this approach is undertaken, beware the all-too-frequent situation where the first question the human agent asks is the one the caller has already answered through the IVR.

Hardest to balance is the cost saving/retention argument. This says that IVR gives you a chance to cut costs even if you can't complete a transaction using only the IVR because it makes the waiting time more tolerable for customers. They are kept occupied pressing buttons on the phone, so they don't notice the wait as much. This means you are less likely to lose them, and also that you can afford to let them wait longer, hence have fewer call centre staff. While there is an element of truth in this argument, it should only be applied if customers can see apparent benefit from the selections they are making. Avoid the vagueness and length of options of some of the menus in the fire station spoof above, and don't keep customers hanging on for more than 30 seconds or so.

Horror story

MSN UK

MSN UK, the British arm of Microsoft's online service, has followed many other UK ISPs by providing free Internet access, in this case hosted by BT. The customer has the choice whether to stay with MSN's old service or use the new 'Freeweb' facility. I recently had the need to ring both the MSN and BT helplines. The experience should have been much the same. They both used the same call charges for help. But compare the experience.

BT – after two rings a person answered. She was able to immediately answer my query.

MSN – after two rings a call management system answered. After a menu asking me how I accessed MSN and another asking what type of query I had, there was a ringing. I then got a message telling me that because of unusually high call rates I would have to wait before I spoke to someone. Then came the baffling bit. There seemed to be a section that was purely for those who connected via Freeweb, yet the very first menu item had established that I didn't use Freeweb at the moment. I paraphrase, but the choices presented to me were something like this.

'If you have problems connecting to Freeweb, please dial [another number]. To find out how to keep your existing e-mail address, press 1. To use your existing e-mail address after migrating to Freeweb, please press 2. To find out how to move back to MSN connection from Freeweb, please press 3. To speak to a technician, please press 4.'

The wording was such that all the options seemed to be about Freeweb. I was baffled and hung on, expecting I could ignore this menu, but no, after a few seconds it was pointed out that I hadn't made a choice. I didn't want any of these options. I wanted to speak to someone about 'classic' MSN access.

The contrast between the two helplines is instructive.

IVR has its uses, but it has extreme limitations. The linear nature of the voice environment is very restricting. A good example is the telephone line of a movie theatre. In a typical multiplex there might be 20 different movies showing in a week. Callers wanting information rather than a booking will tend to fall into two primary categories. They might know what film they want to see, but not the time it's on, or they might want to peruse the list to see what takes their fancy. The first of these requirements is particularly unsuited to a straightforward spoken list. If your customers were talking to a person, they would ask for the times of the movie, not wait until it came up 17th out of 20. If you can't run to a voice recognition system that will let the caller ask for a particular film, it might be worth at least using the letters on the phone keypad to divide the movies into blocks. Even better (for those with access) is a Web site, where that evening's viewing can be scanned with much greater ease. If customers want to know everything that's on, you need to make even greater effort to encourage them towards newspapers and the Web. Even a human operator will struggle talking a customer through every film on show, and the phone line will be tied up for a long time. There might be some mileage in separating the films by category, so someone looking for a horror film or something suitable for children need only listen to the appropriate titles, but it's bound to be a compromise.

Action station

Going to the movies

Ring up the nearest multiplex and see how long it takes you to find out the times of films suitable for children, which are on today.

The nature of the beast

If you are going to go with IVR, there is nothing more important than getting the menus right. Some of this is down to mechanical process work – drawing a neat tree with all the branches properly terminated is essential. You don't want a customer to choose an option only to find that there is no result at the end of it. If the customer then has to press 0 to speak to an agent, the IVR system has become a waste of time and money. It is worth putting plenty of effort into ensuring that this does not happen.

A common problem is that the IVR system is simply too complicated. To avoid caller frustration, it is best to keep the menu structure down to a limit of three levels, each with no more than three choices, which is 27 possible combinations. A 1999 study of over 1,000 North American IVR systems found that the average number of choices was over 70. This is likely to lead to an unacceptable percentage of callers opting out of the IVR to speak to an agent. It has been shown that after listening to seven choices in a menu, 85 per cent of customers can't remember what the first two are.

Even if you get the menu size right, there is something more – assessing the overall feel of the menu for the customer.

Quick tips

A view on IVR

Perhaps the biggest limitation is the bad reputation IVR has with many potential users. This is largely due to a significant minority of truly awful IVR systems in use, with badly structured menus, options that are meaningless and call flows that lead nowhere with no means of returning to the menu. For these there is no excuse.

David Bradshaw, in a white paper for Ovum

In looking for lessons on how to put together a good menu, it is instructive to look at a bad one. Let's pull the humorous fire station example apart.

Thank you for calling the Fire Department. If your school class would like to visit a fire station, please press 1. If you would like to sit in a fire truck and hear the siren, press 2. If you would like to turn yourself in for a recent arson, press 3. If you are a fireman and would like to know what shift you are on this week, press 4. If you recently had a fire and it has started up again, press 5. If you would like to report a new fire, press 6.

Things start fairly well – the introductory sentence isn't too long. But as soon as we hit the first set of choices, there's trouble. It's long. Some of the options are very unlikely to apply to most members of the public, so they would be better hidden away. There is an option for employees, which is a golden error: put employee options on a different phone number. Worst of all, the most important, most urgent option is right at the end of the list.

If you are calling from a business, press 1. If you are at a government agency, press 2. If you are at an amusement park, press 3. If you are in a vehicle, press 4. If you are at a residence, press 5.

The most likely option comes last. What's more, the menu is slipping into jargon. Very few people feel that they are 'at a residence' when they're at home.

If you smell something funny and/or can see smoke and just think there may be a fire, press 1. If you dropped a burning cigarette and cannot find it, press 2. If your car is on fire, press 3. If you are on fire, press 4. If you can actually see the fire, press 5.

A couple of concerns here. One is that this is the sort of menu where you can press too early, because you hear something that approximately matches your requirement. Make sure the structure brings up the clear choices first, with ambiguous options left to the end (if they can't be eliminated). Worse, though, it's the sort of list that makes it very difficult to be sure which option applies to you. Don't put customers into a position where they feel threatened by the choices.

Thank you for reporting a fire. Please enter your five-digit zip code... long pause... You have entered SEVEN-FIVE-TWO-FOUR-FOUR. If this is correct, press 1.

One moment while we open a new case file for you...

Be very careful about making unnecessary or irritating comments. No one wants to be told 'Thank you for reporting a fire' as if they've done you a favour.

If you have called the fire department within the last 30 days, press 1. If you have called the fire department before, but it was not an emergency, press 2. If you have called the fire department before and it was an emergency, press 3. If this is the first time you have called the fire department, press 4.

There are two problems here. First, customers may not know or remember the information requested. Second, it's a set of questions with no relevance for them. Resist the urge to use this type of IVR as a way of collecting customer data, or you will end up with irate customers.

Taken overall, of course, the prime concern is that the whole process has taken much too long. This is a transaction that needs speed and focus, not a gradual filtering down to a result. It also needs a sense of urgency, which the IVR system simply can't convey.

One element of structuring the flow right is to give those with a specific requirement the chance to diverge as quickly as possible. Consider this transaction I recently had with a local multiplex. I had looked up show times on the Web. I knew what I wanted to see and when it was on. I just needed to book the tickets, so I rang the multiplex. The first 20 seconds or so of script suggested that the line was only one for getting information. It was only at this stage that I was told I could press 0 at any time to transfer to the box office. It would have been very helpful to know that up front. In fact I had nearly rung off, so put off was I by the thought of sitting through the listings.

Is there anything more to do? An essential review of your menu structure includes finding the top few likely transactions. What are your callers most likely to want to do? What are your most valuable callers (it's up to you to define 'valuable') likely to want to do? Run through these callers' paths on the menu structure. Is there any possibility for confusion? Is there any way to reduce the number of selections and length of time they have to spend dealing with the menus?

The final stage is external review. It is never enough for the designer of the menu, or even someone else in the same group, to check that the menus make sense. Get someone as far away from your line of business (but as close as possible to your customers) to do it. If this means asking someone's granny or someone's 10-year-old child to check it out, that's fine. Resist the urge to think they don't know what they're talking about. It's not the customer that has got it wrong if your menu is incomprehensible, irritating or difficult to use – it's you.

There is one more check that's necessary, but it is on the IVR equipment rather than your script. It's essential to have the ability to press ahead. The customer should not have to wait until the end of a menu to make a selection (hence the most popular selections being up front). This ability to press the key should be available right from the welcome message, so an experienced user of the system can do so immediately. Ideally, however, press-ahead during the introduction should be suppressed when there has been a major change to the structure, so everyone can hear the part that emphasizes there has been a change. Most IVR systems can now handle press-ahead, but it is best not to assume it's the case without checking.

Talking to a computer

So you've got your beautifully crafted IVR system with a shallow menu tree, an excellent structure and clear prompts. You have a great opportunity to control the costs of a call centre, but you will only reap the benefits if the IVR system is actually used. To deal with old-fashioned rotary (pulse) phones and complex queries, there always has to be a way to bale out and speak to an agent. The bad news is just how often this happens. Recent research suggests that starting with around 30 per cent of customers without touch-tone, you can add another 30 or 40 per cent who simply won't deal with IVR. In most cases between 60 and 70 per cent of your callers will still speak to an agent – and of these a good 60 per cent of the calls could have been dealt with perfectly well by a system. That means half your potential savings have disappeared down the drain.

If it seems that technology is fated not to answer the telephone for you, and you will be forced to resort to a human being, there is an alternative to plain IVR – spoken or natural language IVR. Here the customer does not have to use the telephone keypad, but simply speaks to the computer via the telephone. There are obvious benefits. There is no need for a touch-tone phone (and hence no need for that irritating start to the menu tree, 'If you have a touch-tone phone, please press...'). This isn't such a small advantage as it may at first seem. Although North America, at the time of writing, had only about 25 per cent of wired phones that were not touch-tone (and that's still a fair percentage), other countries had as many as 80 or 90 per cent unable to use keypad IVR.

There are also some dial-up information systems where using the keys from 0 to 9 to communicate with a computer is simply too limiting. Imagine a system with information on each of the US states. Could anyone last through a prompt as far as 'Press 49 for Wisconsin'?

In principle, speech-driven IVR makes it possible to ask a question or give a more sophisticated answer. However, the most basic form of speech-driven IVR simply replaces the keypad with spoken numbers, which can sometimes be a disadvantage. Where you require the customer to enter a number – an account number or a job number, for example – it will take much longer to speak the sequence than to press it on a keypad. And as speech recognition is at best an approximate science, the customer may well have to repeat the number to get it right.

This doesn't mean that simple voice-controlled IVR is always a waste of time and money. It does work where there isn't a touch-tone phone, or where it is inconvenient for the customer to use the keypad while speaking to you. Where the choice is very simple, it also allows for a more natural flow. For instance, the interaction *Do you want to buy shares? [Yes]* is much more natural than *Do you want to buy shares? Press 1 for Yes and 2 for No [1]*.

Getting back to nature

Speech recognition has great potential, but there are problems. It would be very different if you could talk to the computer in the unstructured way in which you talk to a person. That would imply a number of complex features. The system would have to be speaker-independent. It would have to have a good-sized vocabulary and be able to cope with a sentence of continuous speech, rather than a single word at a time. And it would have to be able to have a conversation, changing its expectations of what the speaker was about to say based on the last remark.

This capability is often described as natural language IVR, and is only now becoming a practicality. It has taken so long because it was necessary to evolve powerful enough computers at a reasonable cost, and better algorithms for recognizing speech. Where natural language IVR can be made to work effectively, the potential is enormous. It can deliver almost the same flexibility as a human agent, but at a much lower cost. The interaction becomes caller-led rather than driven by the system. It's win–win, because the caller gets something much closer to a real conversation and is less frustrated, while the call centre benefits too.

One of the benefits is the shortened call flow, which saves money on toll free numbers. Compare these two dialogues, both taking the customer to a share trader in a telephone-based share sales company. This is the natural language version:

*Welcome to OurBank. How can we help you? [I'd like to sell some shares]
You'd like to sell shares. Do you have an OurBank customer code? [Yes]
What is your code? [CL123]*
  I'm putting you through to a dealer.

Compare it with the standard IVR version:

Welcome to OurBank. If you have a touch-tone phone, please press the star key twice. [**]
  Thank you. If you would like to open an OurBank account, please press 1. If you are already an OurBank customer and would like to buy shares, please press 2. If you are already an OurBank customer and would like to sell shares, please press 3. If you have a query about your account, please press 4. For any other requirements, please press 5. [3]
  I am putting you through to a dealer who will ask for your OurBank customer code. Please have your code ready.

Note that the shorter natural language IVR script is actually one stage ahead, having identified the customer's ID. In fact there's nothing to stop the whole of this particular transaction being handled by natural language IVR.

There are other benefits beyond shortened flow for the call centre. There will be fewer calls that have to be passed through to an agent, saving on the biggest call centre cost, and there is an opportunity to put together systems that simply would not have been possible using conventional IVR.

Natural language IVR requires the system to deal with a much wider tree, but customers aren't aware of this – they only see the one branch. That first question in our example, 'How can we help you?', has a vast range of possible replies. The natural language IVR is incapable of dealing with most of them. It couldn't respond sensibly to 'What is the capital of North Dakota?' or 'I've got a headache' unless it had an immense vocabulary and context awareness. However, provided the system can identify just what the speaker is saying, it should be practical for it to handle many of the top requirements, and to ask for clarification on others or send the caller to an agent.

The proviso that the system should be able to identify just what the speaker is saying is not trivial. As recently as the mid-1990s this was a big problem. Speech recognition is hampered by the variations in pronunciation among different speakers of the same language, and the different emphases that individuals make in their speech. Most speech dictation systems require users to train the system to recognize their personal traits. This isn't possible in natural language IVR. Instead, the system has to cope with whatever is thrown at it. As we will see later, it is possible to use a variant on training to fit the system to the customers, but without this there will be problems. In considering the scale of the problem, don't be misled by the numbers that speech recognition companies bandy about.

Modern speech recognition has a success rate of over 95 per cent. If all you want is a spoken digit (for example, a credit card number), this can be pushed up to over 99 per cent. That sounds impressive, but bear in mind that a credit card has between 12 and 16 numbers, each with this error rate. That brings the overall success down to 85 per cent. Customers make mistakes typing a number in on the keypad too. Interestingly, typing a credit card number also delivers around an 85 per cent success rate. However, customers are more willing to believe that they made a mistake typing than they are to accept that the machine didn't recognize their speech accurately.

To minimize possibilities of error, the system will normally have a restricted vocabulary and may need to check meaning with the customer.

Care needs to be taken to avoid forcing the use of words that might prove confusing to the system because other words sound very similar. However, errors will still occur. Under such circumstances, it is best to rephrase the prompt in a way that makes the options more explicit.

A first response after an error might home in on the general direction required. If the system fails to recognize again, the prompt should get more specific still, asking the user to say one of a number of specified keywords. If failure still continues it's time to revert to the keypad or (more likely) pass the user over to an agent. As the errors pile on, the system needs to get more and more gentle with the customer, trying to take as much as possible of the blame on itself. The second prompt might start by saying 'Sorry', while the next might say something like 'I'm really sorry we're having problems', implying that it is the system's fault rather than the customer's.

Just as press-ahead is an essential when controlling IVR from the keypad, it is important with natural language IVR that the customer can speak ahead, either making a selection early in a menu or providing a whole sentence up front that the speech engine can then parse into several choices. To return to the share-selling example, a good natural language IVR system would be able to cope with 'I'd like to sell some shares on account CL123' as soon as the phone is answered.

Implementing natural language

Natural language IVR seems, and probably is, an ideal solution to many call centre problems, but getting it in place is demanding. Given that many call centres will already have some form of IVR, most natural language system developers have opted to piggy-back on to the existing hardware, reducing the need to start from scratch with an installation. This doesn't answer the problem of the scripting. Natural language opens a whole new can of worms in the complexity of the structure.

Good natural language tools enable some mapping to the old IVR structure. For instance, take a question with a 'yes' or 'no' answer, a very simple structure in IVR. In natural language terms, there are well over 100 ways to answer in the affirmative or the negative. A conventional IVR map cannot easily handle each possible answer separately. Instead, the natural language vendors will take any of these answers and provide the appropriate 'yes' or 'no' token for the IVR system.

That still leaves the complexity of a sentence to be dealt with, not to mention handling errors. There is no such thing as a perfect speech recognition system. Accents and dialects can throw the system if it has been set up using a different cross-section of people to those who will use it commercially.

A novel approach to this problem is that provided by Unisys, one of the leaders in the natural language field. Traditionally a system will be set up inside the company and tested by internal volunteers. Over a lengthy time period the programming is modified in response to the results. Gradually more internal testers are brought into the trial. Eventually it is decided that the system is ready to be used by the customers – and all hell breaks loose.

The problem is, however much they try, internal testers aren't real customers. Testers will typically come from a fairly confined socio-economic grouping. Your customers may be more widely spread, or come from different groups. There may be significant regional accent differences between your customers and your employees. And, worst of all, your employees are insiders, and will respond to prompts differently from your customer base.

The bizarre but effective approach Unisys has taken to overcoming this problem is described as a 'Wizard of Oz' technique. In the film of that name, the wizard hides behind a curtain, pretending to be something he isn't. In the Unisys system, an experienced agent listens in on the calls going into a simulator of the natural language system. When a caller responds to a prompt, the response is recorded and analysed, but the action taken depends on the 'wizard'. He or she clicks on the correct result for that particular human response.

There are multiple benefits to this approach. There is no real danger in testing a new system on real customers, because the wizard is always there to untangle any problems. The unexpected customer responses are recorded and learnt by the system as a result of the wizard's intervention. Any failings in the prompts can easily be weeded out, as the wizard observes how the customers respond. If a transaction goes way off track, the wizard or another agent can take over the call and smooth things over. Taking an approach like this to implementing a natural language IVR can make all the difference between success and disaster. (See Appendix 2 for a return on investment model that can be used to investigate the practicalities of natural language IVR.)

Speaking to the Web site

Until recently the only remote access that was possible to a company was over the phone or using conventional mail. With the emergence of the Internet as an international communication medium, more and more companies have jumped on the bandwagon to include e-mail in their communication vehicles and to make the Web one of the prime ways of accessing company information. Any queries that can be pushed on to a Web site result in cost savings, so companies are increasingly getting all the information they can on to their Web sites. In companies where call centres co-ordinate Internet communications (by no means all of them), they have become more contact centres than call centres.

The Web is certainly a superb vehicle for putting information across, but there is a snag. The customer needs to have access to it. This seems so obvious that it's hard to regard it as a real problem, but it is. Your customer base may or may not be at the Internet-aware end of the market. Even in a hi-tech customer base, your customers will only have access to the Web when they can use a browser, linked to the Internet. There are plenty of other times when they can't get this.

A large consortium of IT companies has got together to find a way round this problem. The Voice XML consortium (see www.voicexml.com) has modified the XML language (itself an extension of the basic HTML at the heart of the Web) to cope with voice control. This technology will enable an appropriate Web site to form the basis for a natural language interface. A single source would provide information both to online customers and to phone customers using the natural language IVR. If the products based on this standard prove successful, this could be as big a leap forward as natural language was in the first place.

Hitting the home page

For the Web site, the typical first contact is the home page. This is the shop window of the site, designed to entice customers in or to direct them to the appropriate section they require. Most of the tips for good Web design (see Chapter 5) apply doubly to the home page. It needs to be quick to load, with clear pointers to the places people will want to go. Avoid the temptation to make the home page like a book's front cover – a glossy illustration with the title and little else. This is very frustrating on the Web, and a fair percentage of customers might not even bother to go any further. Get them in and running from the first screen.

Bear in mind, though, that your customers may not come direct to the home page. A search engine (or a bookmark) may bring them to any page on your site. This is probably the strongest argument against using frames on a commercial Web site. Frames look good, allowing the designer to put different Web pages in several boxes on the screen at once. (This means, for example, that you can have a menu down the side or across the top that stays in place when you scroll down the page.) Unfortunately, frames raise a couple of problems. The first is that some browsers (older versions and some of the browsers specially adapted for blind users) can't handle frames. The second problem is that, because each section of the frame is a separate Web page, there is a danger that users somehow get a pointer to just the main text part of the frame without the titles and menus. This will still work in their browser, but they will be disoriented without any context. It's best to manage without frames for this reason. This also means that you should be very careful that, however users come into your site, they can at least get to the home page in a clearly identified way.

Indirect first contact

In the world of the Web, first contact is a strange business because of the interconnected nature of the environment. Someone's first contact with your site could be an advertisement on someone else's site, a simple link or an affiliate site. There's not too much you can do about links (apart from encouraging them widely), but advertising on the Web is a unique proposition that needs careful thought.

It isn't the purpose of this book to develop the theme of how to advertise, but there can be a real danger if your Web advertising isn't driven as much by customer service as by marketing. There are two prime differences between a Web ad and a conventional one. First, the customer pays to see the ad. Unless they have a totally free connection, there is a real outlay as well as the less tangible one of time. This means that you should resist any urge to make your advertising too big and flashy. Waiting a long time for it will not endear you to anyone. This doesn't mean your ads need be boring or static (avoid frenetic, though – it can be irritating). You can get life and interest into a surprisingly small (in download terms) advertisement.

Second, the ad can be more than a banner: it can provide a gateway to your site. For instance, the online bookshop Amazon has adverts on other sites where you can type in the name of a book and an author and you are transported to a search of information about them on the Amazon site. This should be contrasted with a lot of other advertising, which is given the look of something you can interact with – buttons, sliders, meters – but all that you can actually do is click. This is disappointing and deceptive. Remember that a click does not mean commitment; it's easy enough to hit the stop button.

A particularly effective way of establishing remote first contact is through affiliate schemes. There are now thousands of companies running these, and the premise is simple. Other Web sites are given the ability to become mini-franchises, pointing customers at your site, searching your site and linking to specific products on your site. These franchisees add a lot of value to the process. They will spend a lot more effort on their niche aspect of your product base than you will. In return you pay them a commission – usually between 5 and 15 per cent, though sometimes a flat fee.

There is a problem with affiliates, as you are entrusting your first customer contact to people you have very little contact with yourself. Good affiliate programmes put a lot of effort into providing affiliates with easy ways to give the right message to would-be customers. You also handle the contact yourself after the initial introduction, so there's an opportunity to counter any initial problems. Any concern is more than countered by the opportunity to have hundreds or thousands of sites out there moving potential customers, often with a little pre-processing, into your commercial jaws.

Automated e-mail

E-mail has its very own equivalent of automated voice systems, the auto responder. This is a piece of software that looks out for every incoming piece of electronic mail directed to, say, your customer support centre. E-mail is a medium of concealed immediacy. Users expect a quick response, but when they send mail off into the void, they don't really know that it has reached its destination. As it is very unlikely that you are going to be able to respond to the request in minutes, an auto responder gives you an opportunity to say, 'We've got your message; hang on, we'll be back to you soon.' Before thinking about how to do this well, it's worth thinking about whether or not it's worth doing at all.

The trouble is e-mail overload. As a director of one of Europe's biggest insurance companies remarked to me the other day, most electronic inboxes get too much traffic, often from people covering their backs by copying everyone they can think of into a memo. Domestic e-mail users receive trayfuls of unsolicited junk e-mail. Do we really want to add to this irritation with a message that does little more than say 'We aren't doing anything yet'? On balance, the answer is 'yes'. Although many of these confirmations are given little more than a glance and binned, they do provide a strong reassurance that something is happening. That doesn't mean that they can't be improved. Let's look at the anatomy of a typical auto responder e-mail. Corel Corporation of Canada has kindly given permission for me to reproduce one of their auto responder messages.

This is an automated reply to confirm that we have received your request. Please do not reply to this message. This mailbox is answered from Monday to Friday 8:30 am to 5pm (EST).

Thank you for your recent e-mail sent to the Corel Customer Service mailbox.

Due to the volume of mail received, a detailed response to your message may take a while.

For immediate resolution, additional possible venues to explore are:

1. FAQS (frequently asked questions) on our web page concerning common Customer Service issues.

http://www.corel.com/support/customer/tables/table21.htm

2. Contact Customer Service directly at: 1-800-772-6735 (North America only), for issues such as ordering software, replacement parts, pricing/ordering information or the status of your order.

3. Outside of North America, you may contact our International Customer Service Center at: 353-1-706-3912.

If you are writing us regarding a technical support issue, our Technical Services support options can be viewed at:

http://www.corel.com/support/technical/index.htm

For a general listing of our Customer Service and Technical Services telephone numbers, please visit the web address below:

http://www.corel.com/support/technical/howtoreachus.htm

Best regards,

Customer Satisfaction Team

Corel Customer Service

This is by no means a bad auto responder mail. I'd give it around seven out of ten, based on compliance with the following tips for auto responder design.

Quick tips

Auto responder design

- Don't include marketing material. Keep an auto responder to the point, bearing in mind that it isn't actually giving the information that the customer wants.

- Tell customers when they will get a reply. The Corel example doesn't score well on this one, as it is too loose. 'We'll get back to you in two working days' would be better.
- Get back to customers within the specified time. If for any reason you haven't got an answer in that time, let them know what is happening.
- Give customers alternative routes to their requirement. If, as in the Corel example, they have a technical support enquiry, refer them to online technical support options. Give explicit Web addresses including the http://bit: with this, many e-mail readers will let users click on the address in the e-mail and go straight to it.
- Don't be parochial. Although it's a good thing that Corel includes a toll free number for its North American customers, bear in mind the worldwide nature of the Internet. Expecting everyone else to make an international call is just going to irritate them.
- Keep the language upbeat, but don't make it smug or over-effusive. It's fine to thank customers for their e-mail, but don't tell them what a privilege it is to serve them.
- Don't try to pretend there's a real person sending the e-mail. It's made clear up front that this is an automated response. This makes it much better to sign off from a team, rather than an individual.

A final consideration in auto responder design is making sure that your messages are up-to-date. If you are going to include Web links (and I encourage you to do so), you will need to include the auto responder in whatever mechanisms you have to ensure that these links follow the fluid nature of the development of your Web site.

4

Exploration

Customer service is an expensive business. The more you can encourage cus-
tomers to provide their own solutions by exploration, the more cost-effective
your solution is likely to be. This chapter looks at long-distance self-service –
how the best can be better than many personal experiences, and the worst
can be a nightmare.

The appeal of exploration

The aim of exploration is to make it so easy for your customers to sort themselves out that they don't need to bother you. If this can be achieved,
you've got a win–win situation. You win because you save money on the
expensive service you would otherwise have to give. Customers win
because they don't have to talk to you (most of them want an answer, not a
conversation), because they've a sense of personal achievement and
because they may not want someone to laugh at their silly questions.

All too often, though, exploration stresses personal achievement too
highly. We all like to be able to say 'I did that', but if it's buying a book, getting a piece of software to work properly or understanding the electricity
bill, we don't want it to be a major undertaking. The aim should be to put
customers in control of the relationship. They should be able to get where
they want easily and quickly. If it's not practical for them to achieve this for
themselves, it should be very easy for them to escalate from exploration to
help.

What gives the customer control?

The concept of the customer being in control is a powerful one. All the research on stress (see Chapter 14 for more on stress from the agent's viewpoint) suggests that the worst type of stress comes from being out of control. Someone who feels without value and lacking in the ability to influence his or her life suffers most from stress, not someone who has a strong input into what happens. If you can give control of the relationship to customers, allowing them to explore solo as much as they like but giving them the opportunity to turn the exploration into a dialogue with the minimum of effort, you can minimize customer stress and make them feel that yours is a great company to deal with.

That's fine if you can get customers to take control, but how is this achieved? It has to begin with awareness. Until your customers know that they are able to take control, they aren't going to do it. All your communications with customers – advertising, bills, newsletters and magazines, carrier bags, manuals – should have clear pointers to getting going. When your customers arrive at the point of contact, whether it's via a telephone call or online, give them the opportunity to take the reins, and get to the information they want (or buy the product, or whatever) under their own steam.

Good news story

Graphics rule

The face of computers today is very different to that of the early 1980s. Putting aside all the visually attractive features of graphical user interfaces, the biggest impact is probably in the degree of control that has been given to users. Graphical user interfaces have visible menus – you can see what it's possible to do. There are clear controls like buttons to achieve results and there is consistency of look and feel. Contrast this with a pre-graphical interface program. Typically users were faced with a command prompt like C:\> and had to type an instruction with no guidance, and possibly no idea what to do next. Experts were in control. Increased user control has been the biggest benefit of the graphical user interface.

Bearing in mind that being in control means that customers can always call for help along the way, there should be clear opportunities to do this. Online it could be a 'call-me-back' button, but should also include the opportunity to e-mail for help, as some customers are wary of call-back services. On the phone it should be possible to press a key to jump to human assistance. However achieved, the choice should always be with the customer: never drop them directly from exploration to being handled without their say-so.

Starting with the product

In a sizeable subset of customer service interactions you can push this relationship away from the phone or the Web and back on to the customer's own territory. This is particularly true in the area of product support. We have been assuming up to now that customer service implies the customer getting in touch with you, or exploring information at your end of a telephone line or the Internet. However, when you supply a product you can also siphon off part of your knowledge base and put it into the customer's hands. Product design, manuals, online help and self-repairing systems are just some of the ways that you can move the exploration space into the customer's own territory.

Once again we are into win–win. Any exploration that customers do locally minimizes time and space constraints – they can do it when and where they want – and gives the ultimate feeling of control because they do not have to put their heads above the parapet. It is also extremely low-cost as it is available 24 hours a day, 7 days a week for just the initial development cost.

It might seem that topics like product design and online help are far removed from the business of remote customer service, but this very detachment is highly misleading. Unless these elements are seen as part of the overall exploration space, there won't be good enough integration. Just as it should be possible to move painlessly from exploring a Web site to talking to an agent, so there should be an easy transition from exploring a manual or online help to getting on to the Web site or through to the call centre. What's more, the impact on the call centre of integrating these elements into your strategy will be considerable. The only way to keep call centre usage manageable is to get customers to support themselves as much as possible.

Getting the product right

Product design is an immense field, in terms of both the type of products –
we could be dealing with anything from a bank loan through a piece of computer software to a vacuum cleaner – and the complexity of the design process. It is vital that there is dialogue between those responsible for support
and the designers at an early stage.

This may seem a natural requirement, but the history of design indicates
otherwise (see Donald Norman's *The Psychology of Everyday Things* (1988)
for more on the madness of design). With your help, the designer ought to
be asking what can go wrong or what can give the customer the need to look
for assistance. Agents and their managers are ideal people to talk about this.

With a picture of the obvious problems, the designer should then try to
eliminate them from the product. The best help customers can have is to
have problems removed at the outset. This is all down to usability design –
making the controls or other means of interaction with the product trans-
parent in function and easy to operate.

However well the product is designed, though, a level of assistance will
sometimes be required by customers. The next issue is how they can take
the step from knowing they want assistance to finding it. The designer
should always be looking for opportunities to lead customers to assistance,
or even to make the product self-fixing.

Finally there should be convenient delivery of assistance. It is no use
whatever if customers end up being asked to ring a number (half-way round
the world) between certain weekday hours (and it's a weekend). All of this
has to be bundled up into the product design if exploration is to be facili-
tated by moving the starting point into the customer's own space.

No one reads instruction books

Although the old adage that no one reads manuals isn't 100 per cent accu-
rate (a fair percentage of people are avid manual readers), it would hardly
be surprising if it were true. The fact is, most manuals are boring. Manuals
should be enjoyable to read or, even better, they should be eliminated
entirely.

Writing manuals is a chore; and customers don't like using them. Take
computer software as an example of a product where the consumer needs
help. My favourite software documentation is the installation instructions
for one Windows CD ROM. It reads, 'Insert the CD in your CD ROM drive and

wait for the program to load.' That's it. Installation should take care of itself. The product should be so easy to use that you don't need documentation.

Horror story

The dark side of installation

If the Windows documentation described above shows what installation instructions should be like, here's an example of how they shouldn't be. As it's a common problem, the product has been renamed X, but the instructions are real.

Step One
Remove the X CD from the sleeve and place it into the CD ROM caddy with the X label facing up. Insert the caddy into the CD ROM device with the arrow on the caddy pointing into the device.

Step Two
Make a directory (if one does not already exist) to be the mount point for the CD. The following example uses the directory name /cdrom
At your system prompt, type mkdir /cdrom

Step Three
Mount the CD. The following table lists the commands to mount the CD for different systems. The examples assume that you are using the directory /cdrom to mount the CD. You may need to consult your system administrator to determine the proper device name.

A Note on Volume Managers
If your operating environment is configured to use a volume manager, the X CD ROM may have been automatically mounted for you upon the insertion of the CD into the drive, to a file location other than /cdrom. If you are running a volume manager and are not familiar with the volume manager's configuration, please consult your system administrator to determine the CD ROM mount location before proceeding.

Step Four
After the successful mounting of the X CD ROM, type the following commands to change your working directory to the CD ROM mount point and begin the installation. The following table lists the commands to run the installation for different systems.

Table of mount commands
10 commands for different systems, eg mount -r -F hsfs/dev/dsk/cOt6dOs2
/cdrom

To install CD to the mount point: cd/cdrom/setup/X and then type./install*

Of course, one-liner documentation is a simplistic picture. Complex products may need a big, thick manual – but before you assume this, you ought to make sure you've done all you can to improve the usability of the product. Why is it so difficult to use? Your users really don't want manuals. Help should be like medication: it can provide a cure, but it's much better if you can prevent the illness in the first place.

But when you need one...

Sometimes, however hard you try at the design stage, there will need to be a manual or instruction book with your product. It would be interesting to see a survey result about how many companies involve their call centre staff in writing the instructions. After all, they are the people who day after day are faced with complaints about what the customer wants to do but can't, and they should have input into it.

That's not to say that it should be the site's job to write the manual. Getting a professional writer to do it is an essential. All too many manuals suffer from the same problems. The tips below will give some hints on making manuals better, but you can't beat getting a professional to do the writing. What the site should be doing, though, is providing information on the problems customers hit, so they can be incorporated in the manual, and reading through the first draft of the manual to provide critical feedback. This applies no matter what the product is.

Quick tips

Manual writing

- Avoid jargon. You aren't out to educate. If it's easier to refer to something as the twiddly bit on the top left corner, do that rather than calling it the anterior elevation flange unit.
- Don't aim for scientific detachment. Scientific papers go to ridiculous lengths to keep the language objective, but it is not necessary in a manual. Instead of 'It will be observed that the red light flashes', just put 'The red light will flash'.
- Make it readable. Aim for the easy prose of a tabloid newspaper (or a well-written business book) rather than the stodgy writing of a government document.
- Focus on process. Manuals should concentrate on what you do with the product, rather than the structure of the product itself. A software manual that goes through each menu item and says what it is for is next to useless.
- If it's long, have a good index.
- Try not to make it too long.

The thought of producing an expensive manual is sometimes too much for a company, and it resorts to a makeshift production. Take three examples. Bosch is a worldwide manufacturer of household goods, known for excellent quality. The manual for its top-of-the-range US-format fridge/freezer, retailing at 10 times the price of a typical European fridge/freezer, appears to be photocopied, and is a general purpose manual for several different models. It makes a great product look shoddy. Most of the construction manuals for Scandinavian furniture wizards Ikea come in a pictures-only form. That's great for Ikea as they don't need to worry about different languages, but there's only so much you can do with pictures, and the result is often confusion for the consumer. The third example is a camera from a Japanese manufacturer. The English manual has clearly been translated directly from the Japanese, and is sometimes almost incomprehensible.

If you want to save money on manuals, make your products so easy to use that you can do away with instructions. If you have to have manuals, though, don't let your company's image down and make the manual worse than useless by skimping on it. By all means keep it short or use cheap materials to reproduce it, but make it specific, written from scratch in the right language and readable.

Online help

Software is the obvious example of a product with online help, but increasingly anything from photocopiers to phones can have a degree of help built in. The idea is to provide an immediacy of help that a manual can't.

Assuming you've got your documentation written already, you shouldn't just pop it through a clever utility in order to turn it into automatic online help. Imagine what it would be like if TV news was produced by taking stories from a newspaper and slapping them up on the screen for you to read. It is a different medium requiring a different approach. The same is true for help and manuals, which should have a different content too. The manual is there to introduce the product and the tasks it can undertake. Help is there when you don't know what to do next.

You can see this realization of the nature of help in the changes in format of the Microsoft Windows help system, from a clumsy document-based environment to small, crisp statements. Help is more a cue card than an online manual. There are circumstances, of course, where people need help with a task and aren't prepared to go to the manual, but help isn't ideally suited to the role. This is where the wizard concept comes in: if you are helping with a process, active guidance is much more powerful than text. A wizard is part-way between being help and a program – it is help that actively guides you through the task step by step, eliciting the information it needs from you as it goes.

So what is help for? It should answer questions like these:

- I'm told to type my user ID into this box. What does that mean?
- This button says 'calculate'. Calculate what?
- I want to change someone's number in my phone's memory. How do I start?
- I need to print. How do I do it?

But isn't printing a task? It is helpful to think of tasks as what customers actually want to do. They don't want to print, they want to write a letter. Printing is just a sub-task, where help is appropriate. If the task is writing lots of similar letters, the sub-task of mail merge is so complex that it needs a wizard in its own right.

Self-supporting products

The ultimate weapon in reducing the requirement for call centres and online support is to have products that actively help the customer. These are starting to emerge now. There are two broad strands. One involves coping with problems with the product. Cars often have onboard computers that can flag up what is going wrong, though at the moment it usually requires the customer to take the car along to the mechanic's diagnostic computer to find out what is happening. Increasingly the car will be able to interpret this information directly for the customer.

Similarly, from the 2000 version of its Office software, Microsoft has included self-repairing features, enabling a partly damaged piece of software to spot what is wrong and prompt to reinstall the missing parts. More severely damaged software can be given an automatic check-over by the installer software that will replace anything that has been removed or damaged. Once customers have got the hang of using self-maintaining software, for many this will be the first port of call rather than the help desk.

Things don't have to go wrong for the product to provide the user with support, though, and this is the other strand. Again, looking at the Office products, there is an 'assistant', a small moving image on the screen that can be asked for help. This differs from a conventional help system because, like natural language IVR, it is possible to put in a loose question like 'How do I print barcodes on an envelope?' and expect an appropriate answer. Even more sophisticated is the program's ability to spot user behaviour and modify its configuration automatically. For example, if you don't like the assistant and hide it away a few times, the program points out that you've done it several times and asks if you would like it turned off altogether. No need for a phone call or e-mail to ask how to get rid of the thing, the program notes your behaviour and anticipates your implied question.

Current versions of Office are only scratching the surface of this approach. There are still plenty of lost opportunities to offer this kind of proactive help. It could go further in tracking how you interact with the product and watching for ways it could help. But at least Microsoft has made the attempt. Wouldn't it be nice if the cooker spotted that you'd burnt the roast again and suggested a more appropriate temperature/time combination? As long as the customer is in control, such help is valuable, particularly if it can be tuned to the sorts of problem that push customers into using your site.

Once again, then, it is the agents and managers of the call centre and Web site who should be in the front line of pointing out aspects of your products and services that cause trouble and should have support built in.

Getting somewhere

Returning to more conventional exploration, there is one proviso with encouraging your customers to explore: they have to be able to get somewhere. There is nothing worse than spending a considerable effort tracking down a result only to find a standard response that could have applied in any circumstance. For example, I have used Web sites where you follow a lengthy route of questions only to get to a general purpose 'how to contact us' information screen or an e-mail form. Similarly, there are telephone systems where you think that you are going to get the information you need automatically after entering all sorts of data, only to be told that you will now be put through to an operator. The same problem often occurs in online help.

Customers invest time and effort in exploration. The reason they do is that they feel in control of the route to their goal. This feeling of control will be totally shattered if you allow them to run into a brick wall. There is an element of Catch-22 about this. There will be some things that can't be done by exploration, and sometimes you don't know that customers will try to do those things until they're well into the process. However, there are plenty of dead ends that you do know about up front, and it's important that these are flagged up to the customer right at the start. It's much better, for example, that a bank's automatic teller machine, the archetypal self-exploration system, tells you before you even put your card in that it hasn't any cash or has lost its connection to the system, rather than waiting as some do until you've put in your card, put in your PIN and selected your transaction.

Web tools for the explorer

A well-designed Web site is a perfect tool for an explorer. It will have all sorts of routes and mechanisms for getting around. By contrast, navigating some Web sites is more like trying to climb Everest bare-footed, blindfolded and without oxygen. There are some absolute essentials that every Web site should have to make it suitable for exploration. There should be a site search, enabling customers to search the whole site for the information they require. Some form of map helps too. This doesn't have to be a complex graphical design – it could be a simple set of tabs at the top of the screen, with the current location highlighted.

As we have already discussed, the home page has to be an important part of the exploration. It should make it easy to reach any other part of the site. A less-common feature that would also help is for the home page to give some quick process-oriented options (effectively building a manual into the site). Why not have a top 10 'things that people want to do when they come to this site' section with a simple button click to make it happen? Feedback from the queries that are fielded by your agents is essential here. Exploration should feel natural and easy as customers move towards their destinations.

Many sites have 'frequently asked questions' sections. This is a useful part of the exploration support, provided it is approached the right way. Make sure that you do label the section explicitly rather than just using the jargon acronym FAQ. When you get to the FAQ section, remember the poor explorer. All too often there is just a long (long) list of questions and answers that have to be worked through. Give the explorer some form of structure that makes it easy to home in on the appropriate help.

Action station

Your mother should know

If you have a Web site, ask someone from an older generation to find his or her way around it and find out a couple of specific pieces of information. See how he or she manages, what's obvious and what leaves him or her mystified.

Exploring the phone system

Everything that we have covered so far about IVR has involved simplifying and limiting the system, and getting customers to their goal in the minimum time with the minimum of key presses. Exploration requires a different approach. One of the options on the first menu could be designed not to close down the tree but to open it up – an 'if you want to find out more' type option. From there, customers can be guided to different possibilities.

All IVR systems involve a degree of exploring, but they mostly assume that you already know what you want. Imagine a simple IVR that routes you to the appropriate part of the accounts department of a large company. It might say: 'Press 1 for purchase ledger, 2 for accounts receivable, 3 for management accounts, 4 for unpaid bills or 0 to speak to an operator.'

Imagine that you want to query the fact that your invoice to the large company hasn't been paid. You don't know which option you want – you aren't an accountant, and this isn't your jargon. However you don't really want to press 0 and admit to the operator that you are so stupid that you don't know which option to choose. So you dither and perhaps hang up or guess one that sounds as if it might be right and bluff it. To help exploration, there could have been an option 5, 'to get information on the roles of the sections' before being offered the choice again. Such a route makes exploration more practical.

End results – final outcome

If exploration can be made to work well, a large number of trivial queries will be diverted from your site's agents as customers help themselves. This will cut down expensive people-time, reducing the company's costs. It should be good news all round. The customer feels satisfied, and the company has saved money. There is one statistic to be wary of here, though. If your measures of the effectiveness of your site are crude, you will find that performance drops off as exploration becomes more popular. This could go down like a lead balloon with senior management.

The trouble is that the result of exploration is to reduce the number of simple queries to go through to the centre. The corollary of this is that the proportion of complex queries will rise. There will be less traffic, but the average time taken dealing with a customer will rise. If time spent dealing with the customer is your prime measure, you may find that your site's performance appears to drop off. The more you enable exploration, the more important it is to have a balanced scorecard approach to measurement (see Chapter 16).

5

A cry for help

Much of the customer service requirement over the phone and via the Web is for help. It is about support, assistance and information. This chapter looks at the specifics of giving help, over and above the capabilities of exploration.

The last resort

As long as there have been products, there has been need for help to go with them. As we have seen in the previous chapter, help can often be achieved by exploration, but this isn't always possible. Help has two levels of application to supporting invisible customers. The first is providing help for your support system itself, ie help to use your Web site or your phone system. This might not seem necessary, as the assumption is that everyone knows how to use a Web site. It's true that the basic mechanics are generally obvious, but the more sophisticated sites have features that may need explaining, and even if the mechanics are just what you'd expect, there may be jargon involved in your site that needs translating.

A classic example, used as a horror story in Chapter 8, is an experience with the otherwise excellent online investment site Interactive Investor (www.iii.co.uk). This site tells you all you want to know and more about the state of your share portfolio. Specifically, you are told the bid, ask, open and last price on your shares. That's fine if you are an experienced investor, but if you are not, how do you find out what these jargon terms mean? Good online help would mean that by clicking on the column heading you would get an explanation of what the related term means. There is no such feature. Nor is there an explanation in the help section of the site. Just because the terms are an everyday part of your business, don't assume that they are equally familiar to customers.

The second level of help is supporting the users of your products. The best sites provide a whole range of options, which we will explore in more detail later in the chapter. For instance, a site providing help on a piece of computer hardware might have answers to commonly asked questions, downloadable software drivers, a discussion forum and the mechanism to e-mail a question to the support team.

We don't want it

As we saw in the last chapter, you need to bear in mind the fundamental nature of help: it is undesirable, and it implies failure somewhere. If everything worked perfectly, there would be no need for help. As much as possible, through exploration, you will have enabled your customers to sort themselves out. The fact that a call for help still comes through implies that the customer has a serious problem, or desires human contact – or that your self-help facilities aren't good enough. Most sites make gestures towards feeding back problems to the owning parts of the organization, but it is still relatively rare to have a process that makes sure that the problems arriving at a site could have been handled simply using the exploration process if the customer had wanted to do so. You will never get all customers doing it themselves, but they should all have the opportunity to do so.

Web design

When giving help from a Web site, a first consideration has to be making getting to the help as easy as possible. Clear pointers to a generic help function from every page, plus help specifics for your business (for example, driver updates for a computer hardware company), are essential. Further help splits down into help for the process and help for the product.

Help for the process

Sometimes the requirement is not how to use your product, or deal with a problem with your service, but rather 'How do I use this Web site?' or 'What does this mean?' or 'How do I find this information?' Make full use of the interactive nature of the Web. If, for instance, you have a table with column headings that might be jargon, make it possible to click on those column headings to get information on what the heading means. The more interpretation you can have layered underneath items, waiting for the customer to drill down, the better.

You can't assume, though, that the customer will think of clicking on a specific item. Your general help section should include assistance on using the site, as well as on your products and services. An essential part of getting help on the process is the site search. This is a facility, which every site should have, to search the text in the site looking for a topic of interest.

Help for the product

Where a Web site is giving help on the product itself, resist the urge to make the features too glossy. The customer doesn't want to click through 20 beautifully illustrated pages. The need is to solve a problem. A help area should provide as many different possible ways of getting help as possible. This might include e-mailing technical support, a list of frequently asked questions, a how-to section, references on your products and services, and anything else that can add support.

Consider interactive help advisers, which ask a series of questions and try to diagnose a fault, if you can show that a reasonably high percentage of problems will be answered this way. If most customers will find at the end of working through the process that they are not much nearer a solution and still need to send an e-mail to technical support, they will not be impressed with your company.

Call-centre help

For a call centre, giving help is a more direct interaction. While it is possible to give customers assistance with automated menus or fax-back services, most of the time their requirement is to speak to a human being. There is a lot to be said for making this happen as soon as possible, even if the first person they speak to is only responsible for triage.

Phone help – triage

This medical term, first used in field hospitals but latterly used in accident and emergency centres around the world, is very appropriate to the first stages of dealing with help on the phone. In the hospital, a nurse sees patients soon after their arrival at A and E. The nurse's role is to decide which patients need to see a doctor urgently, which can wait a little longer and which can be sent away with minor treatment. In a call centre, the distinctions might be a little different, but the approach is the same.

Ideally, if triage is to be used, it ought to be the first thing customers deal with. If there is an IVR system, that should be regarded as the triage process. The agent dealing with triage (sometimes referred to rather awkwardly as a receptionist) gets customers' basic details and a broad description of the problems. In many cases it may be possible to suggest immediate strategies for solution. Some, though, will need to be referred to a technical specialist.

This is the point at which call centre triage tends to fall down. In passing customers on, the agent needs systems support to be able to pass on all their details, so that they do not have to repeat them all for a second listener. The triage agent needs to have a good enough idea of the workings of the company and its products to be able to direct customers to the right technical specialist. In addition, customers need to be made aware of what is happening, rather than being pushed around as if they had no interest in the matter.

Phone help – talking technicians

Some customers seeking help will end up talking to an expert, someone who knows a lot about your products and services, but who may have no further expertise. What is really needed is expertise in three areas: the technician needs to know your products and services; he or she needs to know about the application of your products and services; and finally he or she needs to know about dealing with people.

Horror story

Driven to distraction

This conversation is alleged to have come from the tape of a support agent for a software company – we'll call it X to avoid embarrassment. The agent in question, fired as a result of the incident, attempted to sue the organization for termination without cause, though the outcome of the suit is unknown. This could be an urban myth, and from some of the detail it's obviously quite old, but it still holds up as a marvellous example of how hard helping someone can be.

'X Technical Desk, may I help you?'
'Yes, well, I'm having trouble with X.'
'What sort of trouble?'
'Well, I was just typing along, and all of a sudden the words went away.'
'Went away?'
'They disappeared.'
'Hmm. So what does your screen look like now?'
'Nothing.'
'Nothing?'
'It's blank; it won't accept anything when I type.'
'Are you still in X, or did you get out?'
'How do I tell?'
'Can you see the C: prompt on the screen?'
'What's a sea-prompt?'
'Never mind. Can you move the cursor around on the screen?'
'There isn't any cursor: I told you, it won't accept anything I type!'
'Does your monitor have a power indicator?'
'What's a monitor?'
'It's the thing with the screen on it that looks like a TV. Does it have a little light that tells you when it's on?'
'I don't know.'
'Well, then, look on the back of the monitor and find where the power cord goes into it. Can you see that?'
'Yes, I think so.'
'Great. Follow the cord to the plug, and tell me if it's plugged into the wall.'
'...Yes, it is.'
'When you were behind the monitor, did you notice that there were two cables plugged into the back of it, not just one?'
'No.'
'Well, there are. I need you to look back there again and find the other cable.'
'...Okay, here it is.'
'Follow it for me, and tell me if it's plugged securely into the back of your computer.'
'I can't reach.'
'Uh huh. Well, can you see if it is?'
'No.'
'Even if you maybe put your knee on something and lean way over?'
'Oh, it's not because I don't have the right angle – it's because it's dark.'
'Dark?'
'Yes, the office light is off, and the only light I have is coming in from the window.'
'Well, turn on the office light then.'
'I can't.'
'No? Why not?'

'Because there's a power outage.'
'A power... A power outage? Aha, OK, we've got it licked now. Do you still have the boxes and manuals and packing stuff your computer came in?'
'Well, yes, I keep them in the closet.'
'Good. Go get them, and unplug your system and pack it up just like it was when you got it. Then take it back to the store you bought it from.'
'Really? Is it that bad?'
'Yes, I'm afraid it is.'
'Well, all right then, I suppose. What do I tell them?'
'Tell them you're too [expletive deleted] stupid to own a computer.'

Misunderstandings like this are widespread enough to become urban myths, and anyone providing support will come across cases of misunderstanding and confusion. There's nothing wrong with finding them amusing, but it's essential that customers do not feel that they are being laughed at. Sympathetic treatment is essential.

Technicians often fall down on the people part of the role. While few customers will be as painful as the one in the example above, there will be a need to deal with difficult customers.

The most important thing is to see problems from the customer viewpoint. If problems can't be fixed on the spot, tell customers just when they will next hear something and what is likely to happen. The key to giving help on the phone is keeping customers' expectations fulfilled.

Web help – the ubiquitous e-mail

E-mail is a natural way to provide help via the Web. The offline nature means that you can handle problems 24 hours a day around the world – there's always a source of help. Providing e-mail help is a must for a business with global customers; without it, you are leaving your customers at the mercy of international phone calls and time zones. It is also a lot easier to manage the flow, so it doesn't have to be such an intensive process as call centre help. What's more, there can be no argument from customers as to what was said on a previous call. As long as you retain the reply, there it is, in the mail.

From the cost per contact viewpoint, good e-mail is a great improvement on telephone communications. It is much easier to route the query to the appropriate people, without the caller remaining on hold while the company gets its act together. Difficult problems can be filtered out and sent to specialists rather than being dumped on the front-line agent. Within reason, the e-mail can be handled when it is convenient for the company, rather than at the moment the customer calls. Of course, there's a price for this flexibility. Without excellent routing and tracking mechanisms for e-mails they can disappear entirely, causing the customer much frustration. But appropriately managed, they are a superb mechanism.

Even so, it is worth bearing in mind that from the human viewpoint, easy to use though e-mail is, it is a second-rate form of communication. If you take the whole spectrum of interpersonal communication, the written word only amounts for a small subset (perhaps 10 per cent) of what you take in. In the written form, it is rarely clear what the emotional content of the text is. You might not think that emotion enters into technical support or sales much, but any interpersonal communication has substrata of emotion, which become obvious when something goes wrong. Misinterpreting the tone of e-mail is a common cause of 'flaming' – sending angry, derogatory mails. It doesn't really help in these circumstances to use emoticons, the rather twee symbols to indicate feeling (eg :-) for a smile), as these look highly unprofessional in a business communication.

Quick tips

E-mail advice

These are some thoughts from an experienced e-mail technical supporter:

> The client often makes a fool of themselves by being overly aggressive in their opening mail (it's so easy to rant at your screen). If your response is cool and considered, the customer (when they are not too embarrassed to reply) realizes how over the top they have been and is suitably humbled. Therefore simply by being polite and helpful, you get the customer on your side. We have several examples where a 'your product is complete crap' mail led, a few exchanges later, to a highly satisfied customer with a personal interest in the product.
>
> Assuming the levels are acceptable, the client's enquiry/complaint – whatever – can be targeted to the right individual to answer. We got lots of positive feedback because our customers were in direct contact with the individual developers. To make the most of this, it's important that the mail comes from a personal mail account rather than a generic one – it gives the customer more faith that they're being taken seriously.

Because you have time to compose yourself before responding, it's much easier to avoid the 'Hey BigCo, your product is crap' – 'So what, customer, your wife is ****ing ugly' urges.

I think response times are crucial. We set up an auto-answer agent, but I try to reply on the day I got a complaint anyway. If you don't, then the e-rant phenomenon really kicks in – 'Hey, I was mad before and now you have ignored me. That makes me really mad.' If you've ever experienced that feeling of disappointment when the postman doesn't deliver the mail you were expecting and you searched forlornly under your doormat in case it experienced some infeasible bounce when it landed, then you'll understand this.

Lastly, I think there is a 'writing to Santa' expectation about sending an e-mail to customer service. Many people were very grateful and often astonished to get a reply – sometimes when it wasn't even helpful.

Making an e-mail work comes down to very careful phrasing of the text. However well it's done, though, some people prefer verbal, visual and touch communication – written words simply don't work for everyone. The ability to read and understand what you have written will vary from person to person, and for that matter from culture to culture, especially if you are communicating with a customer who speaks a different language.

Combine this with the role of junk e-mail at the centre of the whole information overload problem, and the difficulties of creating any sense of responsibility for action, and you can see that e-mail creates a problem for good remote customer service. Does this mean it shouldn't be used? Not at all – the benefits far outweigh the concerns as long as e-mail is used correctly. We will be looking more at getting text communication right later in this section and in the 'Writing skills' section in Chapter 11, but for the moment there are some essentials that need to be considered. Making e-mail a valued part of customer service means keeping negative emotion or implied meaning (anger, sarcasm, irony) out of the text, and ensuring that the context of the mail is understood by those involved.

It's important when using e-mail to communicate with customers that you resist the urge to restrict help to those who have registered or paid for support. It's a classic example of invisible customers getting second-best treatment because of their remoteness. You can't imagine staff in a shop refusing to speak to customers who have not slipped them some cash first.

Horror story

Adaptec passes the buck

Providing help via e-mail is a positive move for everyone concerned. It particularly helps with a worldwide customer base, as customers can record queries and your support team can reply in their own time zones. However, some companies have missed the point, as demonstrated by the help provided by computer hardware manufacturers, Adaptec. To ask a question about their products, you have to have the registration number that comes on a flimsy bit of paper – without it, they won't talk to you.

To make matters worse, as well as producing their own hardware, Adaptec make the most popular software provided with third-party CD ROM writing hardware. This software does not come with an Adaptec registration number, so if you have a problem, Adaptec point you off to the manufacturer of your hardware, even although the hardware manufacturer has much less expertise in the software in question. Adaptec aren't worried about that. If you don't have a registration number, you don't exist. Try to get round the system and they simply ignore your e-mail.

So how do you manage e-mail help? If you have a simple product with little need to get specific details from the customer, the most effective way is just to give the customer total freedom, accepting the unstructured text of a straightforward e-mail message. It isn't just the simplest way to provide e-mail help, but it also feels the most personal. If such an approach would result in too much missed information, resort to a form, but be aware that you are placing a barrier between yourself and the customer.

Quick tips

E-mail forms

If you expect the customer to fill in a form, here are a few tips for making the design practical.

- Don't make the form too long. This is a request for help, not a CV. It's fine to ask for a few pieces of basic customer database information along the way, but don't turn it into a market research questionnaire.
- If you are going to fix the format of data, be very sure about your audience. There is nothing more irritating for a European than filling in a form that insists that you choose a two-letter state code or enter a telephone number in US format.
- Where a piece of information is crucial, try to make it selectable from a list (eg model number), rather than typed in and subject to mistyping.
- It is probably best not to try to emulate wizards. Some forms are split up into multiple pages, advancing a bit at a time. This is the best approach from an interface viewpoint if you have a near-instant connection but if, as is most common, users have to wait 10 or more seconds for each page to appear fully, it's too slow. Keep the form together.

Don't ask the customer for information they can't reasonably be expected to know. For example, it's reasonable for a computer software help form to ask the model of your PC or version of operating system you are running. It is not reasonable to ask the make of the motherboard. If you do need some hidden information, like a serial number, provide help on how to find it.

Once a request for help has been received, use an auto responder (see Chapter 3) to confirm this, and to manage the customer's expectation.

When replying to customers, it is important to get the tone and content right. Thanks to the Corel Corporation of Canada for permission to reproduce this help e-mail as an example.

Hello Brian,

Thank you for contacting Corel Customer Service.

In response to your inquiry, WordPerfect 6.1 was designed and tested for use on the Windows 3.1x platform. There may or may not be certain issues with your WordPerfect 6.1 if you choose to run it on Windows 98; it depends on your particular system's configuration.

WordPerfect Office 2000, however, was designed and tested for use on Windows 95 and 98.

For more information or to order software please call the Customer Service Center nearest you. In North America the phone number is 1-800-772-6735. To obtain the telephone number of an International Customer Service Center, please visit our web site at:

http://www.corel.com/support/customer/tables/table21.htm

You may also purchase Corel products online at Corel's eStore or visit a local reseller. For more information, please review the website below: http://www.corel.com/shop/index.htm

I hope this helps to clarify things!

Customer Satisfaction Team
Corel Customer Service
customerservice@corel.com
Www.corel.com

Please attach previous message for future reference.

Brian Clegg wrote:

> Hi – I've got a copy of WordPerfect suite for Windows 3.1 (the one with
> WordPerfect 6.1 in). I'm upgrading to a new PC with Windows 98. Will my
> existing WordPerfect suite work okay? If so, is there any advantage in
> upgrading to a more recent product?

> Best regards,

> Brian Clegg

In responding, there are a number of points to watch out for:

1. Keep an audit trail. In Corel's e-mail my original request was included. If I then replied, although the e-mail would be growing quite long, it would be possible to keep track of exactly what had been said by both parties.
2. Be friendly. Most people now find a greeting like that at the start of the Corel e-mail more pleasant than 'Dear Mr Clegg' or, even worse, starting with no greeting at all. There are some groups for whom this is not true – if, for example, your customer base is largely elderly, you might not want to launch into first-name terms.
3. Resist the urge to go into sales mode. The Corel e-mail is borderline in this respect. The vast majority of products for Windows 3.x run fine with the more recent version of Windows. It might have been more helpful to say that, while it's always possible something could go wrong, it's worth a try as it won't cause any damage, and if there are problems, I should move to the newer product. It would be quite acceptable to point out other advantages of the new product to make the cutover more worth while, provided it doesn't turn into a major sales pitch.

4. Give help with what to do next. The contact information is useful here, though non-North American customers might find the particular approach rather chauvinistic. As with an auto responder, having full Web addresses (including the http://) is a good idea, as it means customers with modern e-mail software can click on the address and go straight to it.

5. Something missing from the Corel e-mail is the end of the last sentence. Rather than 'I hope this clarifies things!' it would have been better to have said, 'I hope this clarifies things – if not, get back to me for more information', putting the closure of the conversation into the customer's hands.

6. Another 'could do better' here is the sign-off. While it's entirely valid to send an auto responder message, which is impersonal, from a team, a specific answer to a problem like this has come from a person. Note the use of 'I' in 'I hope this clarifies things!' It would be significantly more effective if it was signed by a person, with that person's e-mail address as the return address. This emphasizes that it is a personal service and, should something go wrong, I would be able to keep up a dialogue with an individual rather than a faceless team.

It is worth expanding on a couple of those points. The first concerns keeping away from sales mode. It is very tempting. After all, here are customers having problems with a product – a great opportunity to sell them a new one. But the motivation you are giving the customers is all wrong. Would you rather have someone buy your product because the old one doesn't work, or because you give such great service? It is not great service to bombard customers with sales literature when they ask for help. It makes it look as if the company isn't listening.

The other significant point is the use of personal e-mails. The practicalities of this can sometimes get in the way of the vision. It's easy to think, 'But what if a particular agent gets snowed under, or goes on holiday, or leaves the company?' You can, if necessary, cheat slightly. Customers don't know who is sitting at the keyboard.

Don't cheat all the time, though. A TV consumer-affairs show recently attacked an insurance company where every customer services letter was signed with the same name. Unfortunately, anyone getting more than one letter got totally different versions of the signature. It's fine to stand in for another agent, but not so good to apply this approach to a large-scale operation.

Another concern is that customers will hang on to the individual e-mail addresses and use them inappropriately. This is less of a problem than it might seem but, even if someone does, it's easy enough to have a fairly standard (if personally signed) response saying that, to make sure all queries are handled as fairly as possible, it is necessary to use the standard channels to send in an initial query. This assumes you are inundated. If things are quiet, why not answer? Having a personal relationship is what great customer service is all about.

Web help – call me

An attractive option that is appearing more and more on Web sites is a 'call-me-back' button. The initial response to these was suspicion. Just as people were initially wary of buying from Web sites but gradually came to realize it was a safe and convenient way to do business, so a lot of people hold off clicking on the 'call-me-back' button. The trouble is, it involves putting your head over the parapet. While browsing you can feel anonymous and invisible, with the reasonable assumption that someone isn't going to jump out of a corner of the screen and say, 'I know what you're doing.' Once you click on one of these buttons, it is as if you are saying, 'Here I am, look at me!'

There's good reason to encourage the use of 'call-me-back' buttons. However, companies don't always know what to do with them. Unless your environment is slow-paced, it isn't enough to rely on receiving an e-mail and manually making a call. The sooner you react to a request, the more chance there is of turning an enquiry into business – and of satisfying the customer. According to the 1999 report, 'Next Generation Call Centres: CTI, Voice and the Web' by European analysts Ovum, anecdotal evidence suggests you have anywhere between a 40 per cent and a 200 per cent better chance of getting customers' business if you can call them while they are still on your Web site. For domestic users with a single phone line this is not possible (though you could call their mobile phone – it is surprising how reluctant businesses are to do this even when 'big ticket' sales are involved), but with business customers there is normally no such limitation.

Horror story

We can't talk to you

The UK motoring organization AA has a lucrative line in insurance sales. Their Web site is set up to give an instant quote but, as is usual with insurance, there is a range of provisos that should be met if you require a quote. If anything in this checklist doesn't fit your circumstances you are asked to dial a toll free number – or to click to be called back.

So far, so good. The call-back screen is easy to use and includes a helpful item that is not always included – a pull-down box allowing customers to select when they want to be called back, with a range of options from 'in the next two minutes' through to 'in 30 minutes'. When I tried the service, the phone rang within seconds of clicking the button. However, when I spoke to the agent, she said that she was unable to handle an insurance quotation, and I would have to ring the toll free number. So call-back, instead of being a helpful adjunct to the site, was in this case an irritation, which wasted everyone's time with no benefit.

The AA example shows that even with fast call-back, you can get it wrong. Having a good match of the promise of what you intend to deliver on the Web site with the reality of your service is essential – and having a call-back mechanism that can't link into your ordinary sales routine is pointless. Making best use of call-back requires a very careful analysis of the processes the customer is likely to go through.

What is becoming increasingly clear is just how much has to be got right to make remote customer service work. In the next chapter, we look at one of the least easy to pin down, but most powerful, contributors to the customer relationship: getting the glow.

6

Getting the glow

There is more to customer service than the content. This chapter looks at the difference between just giving the customers what they ask for and sending them away with a warm glow about your company.

The glow

Customer service isn't just about what you deliver, but how you deliver it. Anyone can give you the right product; only special customer service agents can give it to you in such a way that you feel they're pleased to serve you, and are genuinely interested in you. Getting that glow of appreciation is the real aim of dealing with invisible customers. You don't just want them to like the products, you want them to go away and tell their friends what a great service they got from your company. In many ways this is easier to do for a small company than a large one. In a small company the customers are known individually. The agent knows what they are worth to the company and how best to treat them. Customers probably know the agent personally and feel they are dealing with a friend. For a large company, getting this small-company feel is an important part of getting the glow, and we will return to it in several other chapters.

Good news story

Check this out

This example of getting the glow actually took place at a supermarket checkout, but it would work equally well on the phone. The location was somewhere in New York State.

> A little while ago, in our small downtown supermarket, I was at the checkout. The sales assistant paused as she put one of the items through the scanner. "That's cool," she said, "I haven't seen one of those before. They're amazing value, aren't they? I'll have to get one myself." It made me feel good.

Two things were happening here. The agent was indirectly complimenting the customer on her choice, and was giving an 'insider' view that the product was good value. The customer got a glow from this aside. There is a small risk in a hi-tech environment that the customer will be concerned that the agent doesn't know about a product, but generally this approach (if not over-used and made mechanical) will be very effective at giving the glow. Make sure, though, that the product is one that could genuinely elicit such a response, even if it isn't a genuine one for this agent. Being apparently pleasantly surprised about the existence of a common everyday item ('Gee, a paperclip – what a neat idea') or gushing about a new product that simply isn't inspiring ('Isn't this brilliant? Having an extra slice of ham in the packet – I'd never have thought of that. I must get some myself') is immediately false and destroys the illusion of having a genuine conversation.

What makes the difference?

It would be nice if this glow could be generated by a system and a formula. There are many companies leaping on to the electronic commerce band-wagon and emphasizing how their system lets you build flexible scripts and manage customers efficiently. These products are fine, but using them alone would miss the point. Getting the glow is about making the customer feel special, which won't happen if you use a script to make sure that the interaction with each customer is just the same.

The trouble that remote customer agents face is that they lack one of the principal tools of the good glow-giver – non-verbal communication. Take this example that happened to me in a supermarket restaurant recently.

There were two people serving. The first made me feel as if she was pleased that I was there, by smiling, not just when I went to the till, but the two or three times we passed each other in the restaurant. The second wore a scowl that said, 'Talk to me if you dare.' I made the mistake of asking her for a fork, as the nearby bin was empty. 'There are some at the far end,' she said, pointing down the length of the restaurant. 'There aren't,' I said, 'I've already looked.' She seemed put out. 'There's another lot on the other end of the display,' she said. 'That's empty too.' With no further response but a loud 'tut' she disappeared into the kitchen. I felt obliged to shout after her, 'You are supposed to say sorry.' She appeared not to hear me.

Making the difference between these two extremes requires very little effort, but so often it doesn't happen. It's hard to believe that coming across well to the customers was high on the list of requirements of whoever recruited this person. Maybe a 'glow factor' assessment would have helped. However, the point of this illustration is the importance of the non-verbal parts of the customer service role. Even without our fork debacle, there was a totally different feeling, all down to facial expression and body language. What if you are dealing with customers on the phone, or through a Web site?

On the phone, you might not be able to see the other person, but at least you have got speech on your side. Speech is much less powerful than body language in getting a gut-level message across. If you doubt this, try telling someone you like his or her clothes while shaking your head and see which is believed. This low emphasis on speech means that you have to work extra hard at the nuances that say 'welcome' in your voice. This isn't the same as being gushing and effusive. The glow comes from the same things that distinguish a phone conversation you enjoy from one that makes you feel uncomfortable. We'll look at this in more detail later in the chapter in the 'Speaking the glow' section.

The Web site can only do so much to be 'friendly'. In the end, the glow almost always comes from an interaction, rather than a broadcast. At the moment, at least, Web sites don't have the multimedia muscle to put across an emotion the way a feature film or a good TV show can, nor is there the time to develop an emotion. Instead, you are dependent on your interactive features, typically e-mail. There is more on this in the 'Mailing the glow' section below, but the key factors have to be provision of a personal rather than an automated response, and positive, warm human language rather than legalese or stilted business-speak. Before we look at injecting that glow, though, it's worth considering how customers themselves can make things difficult.

Horror story

The customer is always wrong

It's sometimes too easy, especially in a technical setting, to assume that the customer has got it wrong. This example shows how an agent can misread the circumstances by always assuming this to be the case.

I recently had a problem with my e-mail. I could send e-mails and access the Internet with no problem. However people who were trying to send me e-mails received the message from CompuServe that my user address was invalid. Therefore, no e-mails even reached my mailbox.

When someone rang to tell me of this, I contacted the CompuServe help desk. Most of the staff there are reasonably well informed and helpful. That day however an obviously ill-informed young man, whose perception of customer service left much to be desired, advised me that the fact that their server was refusing to recognize my user name and accept e-mails for me was nothing to do with CompuServe! The problem lay with my PC and that I should have it checked out!

Fortunately some of his colleagues were less disinterested and the problem was solved. But I was appalled that someone with so little knowledge of the service and who clearly had no idea that there is a wide choice of ISPs out there was even allowed to answer the telephone! The conversation I had with this young man enraged me even more than the considerable inconvenience of having to contact all my customers to apologize for being offline for two days!

Stupid customers

Anyone who has provided customer service, particularly around a hi-tech area, will have some tales of 'stupid' customers. Generally speaking, your customers know less about your business than you do, which is hardly surprising – what is meat and drink to you is a casual purchase or a small part of life to them. Of course, they aren't stupid, but you will have to advance with caution if you are going to maintain that glow.

Let's make it clear the sort of thing we are dealing with. When I managed the PC centre at a large corporate, I had a very worried secretary ring me up. 'I've heard about these computer viruses,' she said. 'I wouldn't worry for myself, but I'm having a baby. Is there any danger of me catching one?'

Before my time in the PC centre, when the most common type of diskette was the large, flexible 5¼ inch floppy, stupid customer incidents were rife. There was the person who pushed the disk into the gap between the two drives, the person who folded one double to go into an envelope, and the person who stapled accompanying documentation to a diskette.

Such mistakes and confusions are funny, and it's human nature to appreciate them, but to maintain good customer service you are going to have to take a few practical steps:

- Don't spread the story everywhere. It's impossible not to tell someone about howlers like these, but most particularly, don't spread them in such a way that versions of them can get back to the people who made the errors, with names attached.
- Don't treat the person involved as if he or she is an idiot. No one is an expert in every subject.
- Such mistakes are rarely wilful stupidity, but usually result from a misunderstanding. Don't just fix the problem, but improve the understanding.
- Be reassuring and supportive. Whether or not you think so, say that you understand the mistake.
- See if there are any lessons to carry forward. If the same mistake happens more than once, you may be seeing signs of a widespread misapprehension in your customer community. Can you educate them out of it or, even better, change whatever is causing the confusion so that it is no longer a problem?

Perhaps the most important thing to bear in mind when dealing with such customers is that they may be well aware that they appear ignorant. Just because you don't know something doesn't mean you don't know that you don't know it. Reassurance is all-important in such circumstances. In particular, see if you can shift the blame away from the customers. Tell them everybody has problems with it (whatever it is). Feel free to blame technology if it helps – not as an excuse for you having made an error, but if fear of technology is making the customer feel ignorant.

Taking the blame yourself is important too. If the problem is your fault, say so and apologize. Don't give the customer the run-around. Make sure everyone employed in customer service understands this point. Bear in mind, though, that if you are in a position where the customer's reason for using your services is your technical expertise, it's probably not a good idea to try to put the customer at ease by saying, 'It's not surprising you find it confusing. I don't understand it either.' It doesn't foster customer confidence.

Difficult customers

It's not so bad when the customer simply doesn't understand, but there's another class of customer where giving the glow is an uphill battle: the unreasonable customer, who isn't prepared to listen or to be constructive.

Horror story

Mr Angry

This story, in an agent's own words, is from a call centre in Dallas, Texas. It is all too typical of the irrational behaviour that agents sometimes have to cope with. The conversation involves a modem (one of the devices used to connect a PC to the Internet over the phone) and an Internet Service Provider. The modem in question was labelled 56k, suggesting that it could handle 56,000 bits per second (actually 57,344 bits per second). As John, the agent at the ISP, tells the customer, this is not the reality when using such a modem.

Phone rings...
Me: This is John, how may I help you?
Customer: I have a 56k modem, but I only connect at 45,333. Are you guys having some kind of problem?
Me: No, sir, that's not a problem; that's about an average connect speed.
Customer: What do you mean an average connect speed? What's the problem over there? When are you going to upgrade your equipment?
Me: Sir, we have state-of-the-art 56k equipment. It's made by Nortel. FCC regulations prevent you from connecting at a full 56k. Not only that but the technology is limited by the quality of your phone lines.
Customer: Well, there's nothing wrong with my phone line!
Me: You must have a perfectly clean line to get a significantly higher connection speed. Very few people have such a line.
Customer: My friend across the street connects to his ISP at 57,600. I think you guys need to get it together up there.
Me: Sir, that speed that he is seeing is not the speed at which he is connecting to his ISP, that's the speed that his computer is connected to his modem. Modems can report two different speeds, but your computer can only show you one of them. The speed that you see is determined by the way your modem is set up.
Customer: Well, that's bull crap. You're just giving me the run-around!
Me: Sir, I know sometimes this can be very frustrating. But you really are connecting quite well. You simply don't understand how all this telecommunications stuff works.

Customer: Don't tell me I don't know how this stuff works, I'm an engineer for GTE.

Me: (thinking 'Oh, my God') Well, sir, if you are not happy with the service, I'll be more than glad to refund you your money.

Customer: I don't want my money back, I want you to make this work!

Me: Our equipment is running fine. There's nothing more I can do for you.

Customer: Well, that's bull crap. You guys probably have something configured wrong!

Me: Sir, I configured everything myself; I know it's working properly. If it were not configured right, it wouldn't work at all.

Customer: You must be pretty stupid then.

Me: Look, I've had it with you. I explained to you what the deal is and you can't accept it. I'm not paid to kiss your ass! What's your name so I can have your money refunded?

Customer: I don't want my money back, and I'm not giving you my name. I am paying you to kiss my ass, so get off of your ass and fix the problem!

Me: You know something, I can find out who you are from the caller ID logs, and trace that back to your account. When I find out who you are, I'll make sure that you do not get a refund at all, and your account will be closed anyway! Have a good day!

I did find out who it was, and I did close his account. I never heard about the guy again; I don't know if he called my boss and got a refund or not. I don't care, but this story really sticks in my mind.

It's easy to say that the Dallas agent in the horror story above over-reacted, but there is no doubt that the conversation got out of control, and some form of drastic action was necessary. It may be that one of the quick tips below would have helped him out, but there are some circumstances when you aren't going to win and you might as well cut your losses.

Quick tips

Difficult customers

There isn't a magic solution, but these tips might help:

- Try to maintain an even, reasonable tone.
- Don't be patronizing – you will just make things worse.

- Explain any technical problems in non-technical terms.
- Try to put yourself on the same side as the customer. The agent in the horror story says, 'I know sometimes this can be very frustrating.' Take it even further – in this example he could have explained how modem manufacturers mislead the public by using these numbers.
- Don't tell customers they are stupid. The biggest mistake the agent made in the horror story was to say, 'You simply don't understand how all this telecommunications stuff works.' At once the customer was offended, especially as he considered himself a technical expert.
- If customers don't believe you, try to refer them to an independent source they might trust. In the horror story, it might have been worth referring the customer to a trusted computer dealer, the telephone company or even the modem manufacturer.
- Don't close down too early. When the agent said, 'There's nothing more I can do for you', he challenged the customer. It's a pain, but as much as possible you need to let the customer be the one to shut things down.
- Don't react to insults. It won't help anyone.
- Don't threaten customers.

If customers won't close down, you will eventually have to do it. Apologize, tell them that it seems you aren't able to do anything and refer them to your customer complaint procedures.

The key to keeping up the glow through a verbal assault by the customer is maintaining a cheerful (though not humorous) stance. Managing the tip about not reacting to insults is at the heart of this. It's a lot easier to say than to do. As the customer becomes more irate, your stress system will kick in. There's more detail on stress management in Chapter 14, but for the moment it is enough to be aware of what is happening. Your automatic responses will judge aggressive speech as a threat and push you into fight or flight mode, pumping adrenalin and other hormones into your system. You aren't going to run away (probably), so you will begin to fight back, and then you've lost it.

A few simple techniques will help. Take a couple of slow, deep breaths. This will help counter the stress and will give you a chance to come up with a measured response rather than a reflexive one. Try to sympathize with the customer's problem. Remember that he or she has got a problem; it is just out of proportion or misinterpreted at the moment. Force yourself to smile. It doesn't matter that the person can't see you – you can't help relaxing some of your aggression when you smile. Most of all keep the whole thing in perspective. What does it really matter? Enjoy it rather than suffer it. Imagine it's Victor Meldrew or another irascible TV character. Let it wash over you, and then return to your measured response.

The long view

Although the idea of a 'glow' implies short-term impact, one of the best ways to establish that glow is to take a long-term view. Earlier on we established the idea of a lifetime value. It's simply not appropriate to think of customers only in terms of the value of the transaction you are currently undertaking. Whether or not you give them the glow may well make the difference between keeping them for years, with many more transactions, or losing them today.

Good news story

Putting off the customer

This is a story from a conventional shopping environment, but the lesson is entirely valid for call centres and Web sites. I went into the camera store in the nearby large town and asked what was now available in digital cameras for around £400 ($600). The answer was shocking at first. 'I wouldn't sell you a camera in that price range,' said the sales assistant. I was about to ask him what was wrong with my money when he went on. 'One of the best manufacturers has just dropped the price of its cameras from £650 to £400. If you come back in a few days, I can do you a much better camera for £400 than I could today. I really wouldn't recommend buying anything now.'

Look at what he did. He turned away the chance to make an immediate sale. Taken in isolation, it is madness, and sadly it's something that the sales assistants in many chain stores (and call centres) would not do, because it's push, push, push to move goods today. What the assistant did was to balance the value of the sale now against my long-term custom. I was very impressed that he had said that he wouldn't sell me a camera now, and that by going back in a few days I could get a much better one. I will go back, not just for that camera but for other purchases. And I have already passed on this story to several other would-be purchasers.

In the example above, the sales assistant took the long-term view. He gave me the glow, by putting a consideration of my benefit above an immediate sale. Of course, he has actually vastly increased the potential revenue his company makes from me and from the people I have recommended them to. But taking that action meant that he had to be prepared, and allowed, to take a risk. See Chapter 12 for more on risk-taking.

Giving a glow is often about thinking longer term. How much might this customer mean to the company over the next year? How about five years, or 10 years, or 25 years? Lots of companies think that their reward schemes, giving discounts to regular shoppers, are enough to ensure loyalty in the long term, but are they really? Isn't it time to consider doing your best to get the customer the best deal, even if you lose out in the short term? After all, brand loyalty is on the wane. Consumers are more and more inclined to shop around.

Action station

Don't buy from us

Consider your reactions to the following short scenario. A customer rings the SuperFund insurance company's call centre and asks for a specific household insurance. The agent says, 'I can sell you that, and our insurance is very good, but I ought to point out that, just for this week, our competitors, HappyHomze, have a special on that's 20 per cent less than ours. Could I note down your details anyway, because in a year's time when you come to renew, we'll be cheaper and better than HappyHomze, but just now I think you might be better buying from them. I can give you their number, if you like.'

- As this agent's manager, what would your reaction be?
- As the customer, how do you feel about SuperFund?
- If the SuperFund agent had not mentioned the HappyHomze deal and you found out about it just after you'd signed up with SuperFund, how would you feel?
- If you needed more insurance, would you be inclined to try SuperFund first?
- Would you be likely to tell an anecdote about your experience to your friends, recommending SuperFund?
- When SuperFund called in a year's time, would you take their proposal seriously?

Taking a long-term view in business is difficult. Books have to be balanced and shareholders mollified this year and every year. But without that long-term view, you are unlikely to sustain a long-term company. Remember the airline with the missing nuts (see Chapter 2)? The lifetime value of a customer will usually far outweigh any single transaction. Giving the glow is incompatible with short-termism.

Reassurance

If the customers are to feel that you are giving them great service – to really get that glow – they need to feel comfortable. Part of the process of making them comfortable is about reassurance. Human beings like feedback and closure. They like to know what is happening in a process, and to have the certainty that a process they have started has been brought to a satisfactory conclusion. Without feedback and closure, we become uncomfortable and regard the process with suspicion. It's the need for feedback that has resulted in all the pretty thermometer-like bars you see in computer software that tell you how far you are through a process. Producing such progress bars may actually slow the process down, but it's worth it to have the reassurance that something is happening. You can't look into a PC and watch the process in motion. If there is no feedback, or something as static as an hourglass, before long you suspect that everything has gone wrong and start to pound on the keyboard.

Remote customers have exactly the same problem. You can't see them and, most importantly, they can't see you. They don't know if you have understood just what it is they want. They don't know if you are doing anything about it or have just put their file on a huge pile in the corner of the office. The problem or the purchase or whatever reason they have for contacting you might be crucially important to them, but they will assume that you consider it to be unimportant. Worst of all, if they don't hear anything from you, they will assume that nothing is happening. The only glow they are likely to get is from their growing irritation, as (apparently) nothing happens.

To ensure that you do not fall into this trap requires a steady flow of communication. To minimize the feeling that you don't understand the requirement, it is important to feed back to customers exactly what you think it is. From a call centre, this might mean summarizing what you think you've heard, so customers can check it against what they *know* they've said. When communicating by e-mail, it will help to keep the customer's original message attached to the reply. Automated Web systems need to flag up that requests have been accepted for action – so, for example, when books have been ordered from Amazon.com, customers receive a confirmation e-mail in a few minutes that tells them what has been ordered, what it will cost, where it will be delivered to and when they can expect it. It also tells them, right up front and not in the small print, how to do something about it if the order is wrong.

At this early stage of reassurance your main role is managing expectations – giving customers a clear picture of just what they can expect you to do (and if relevant, what you expect them to do). Following that, we are into the waiting period. If it is longer than a few days, it makes sense to report on the status of the job and if relevant any actions required from either side. This is the equivalent of the moving bar on the PC – you are letting customers know something is happening. If you know for certain that nothing will happen for six months, it doesn't make sense to have updates every few days confirming that nothing has happened. Under such circumstances it is quite acceptable to say, 'Nothing will happen for six months. We will get in touch on date X to bring you up to date', but in most circumstances regular updates are valuable.

Finally comes closure. Just because you've ticked a task off it doesn't mean that customers have. Again, Amazon.com sends out a message saying that the product has been dispatched, when and how it was dispatched and when it is likely to arrive. Customers are told what to do if it doesn't get there. Make sure that customers know that you've finished, and give them the chance to tell you that they don't regard the matter as closed.

That's fine, of course, as long as you have actually succeeded. Sometimes you can't help. It might be that you know this up front. Customers might have come to the wrong place, or the requirement might be beyond your capabilities. If that's the case, tell them straight away. If possible, point them towards someone who can help, making that as simple for them as you can (remember long-term thinking: it makes sense, even if it means pointing them at a competitor). What is absolutely disastrous in these circumstances is doing nothing. After all, no one likes to admit to failure. But the negative impact of this approach is too great. Don't leave customers to work out what has happened by themselves. The same applies if there is failure part-way through a process. It might be painful, but the sooner you can make customers aware, the better the chance of recovering from the disaster.

Service recovery

Things go wrong. There is no such thing as zero defect. When an aspect of your service fails, you are at a particularly dangerous point in the relationship with customers. You can lose them, losing not only a one-off sale, but all their lifetime value. Worse, bad service is something people like to talk about. It wouldn't be exaggerating to say that one example of really bad service will result in at least 10 people knowing how bad the service was and being encouraged to avoid your company in the future.

However, provided failure isn't too regular an occurrence for a particular customer, it is possible to realize the cliché and make a problem into an opportunity. If you can accept something has gone wrong and put it right in such a flamboyant way that the customer will be telling his or her friends not how bad you are, but how great you are, it is possible to turn a defect into an advantage. This is the concept at the heart of service recovery, but the trouble is, like other concepts of good service, it is more often talked about than provided.

Horror story

Failed recovery

Here's a US example of an attempt at service recovery that compounded the original problem.

Last fall I was flying down to Miami to give a presentation at a sales conference. I intended to stay on a few days, so unusually I had a bag in the hold. The flight from Washington was packed, and late. When we arrived, my bag had disappeared. I had my presentation in my briefcase, but all my clothes and a valuable set of samples were in the bag in the hold. I went to the X Airlines desk.

The woman at the desk was sympathetic. She got me to fill in a form. I then asked what she was going to do about the fact that I had nothing for my stay – no clothes, no wash bag. She apologized profusely, but explained that it was company policy not to provide emergency stop-over kits on internal flights. Whatever I said she would not move – she had no authority to act. I bought my own.

Nearly five months later I received a check from X Airlines for an arbitrary sum that is apparently the standard rate for lost baggage. The amount wouldn't even pay for the suitcase. Up to then I was a regular flyer with X Airlines. I used them at least once a month. I won't be any longer.

In the horror story above, the airline had a procedure for dealing with lost bags, a service failure that the airline industry has plenty of experience with. The whole procedure is designed to protect the airline, not to make the passengers feel it wasn't such a bad experience after all. There were two chances to provide service recovery, neither of which was used.

This passenger was stuck 900 miles from home without a change of clothing or a wash bag. The first opportunity was to provide the customer with an emergency kit to keep him going until his case turned up, or he had a chance to get some other clothes organized. This particular airline did have such a contingency measure – but only for international travellers. It didn't matter to this passenger whether his flight was internal or not – he just wanted to be sorted out. The agent appeared to have no flexibility in the way she responded.

The second opportunity came later, to compensate the passenger for the loss and make sure he realized that the airline cared. Five months was much too late for this. An initial response should have come within a day or two, and the whole matter should have been settled within a fortnight. Anything more and recovery becomes very difficult. The crowning glory of this failure to recover was the trivial compensation – 'the amount wouldn't even pay for my suitcase'. The minimum amount of compensation an airline has to give for a lost bag is governed by an international convention, but there is no reason why it cannot increase the amount.

How could things have been better? The agent should have been allowed the discretion to realize that this was a case where it would have been sensible to provide an emergency kit – and more. If she had said, 'Is there anything else I can do to help?' and the customer had requested, say, a car to take him to his hotel, that should have been within her discretionary powers. Unless the people on the ground have the flexibility to spend money and make something happen, recovery is doomed. As for the compensation in this case, the customer should have received a fair replacement value for the contents – and, to really give the glow, a free ticket to a vacation destination thrown in.

To be able to respond in this way and turn disaster into triumph, two things are needed: trust in the agent, and an awareness of the customer's value to the company. We'll look at trust more in a later chapter. For the moment, it's enough to say that companies who do give their front-line employees the right information, training and trust find that they can allow them huge latitude – perhaps several thousand dollars – to make service recovery happen successfully. Employees use this ability sensibly on the whole. It works.

The awareness of value is the crucial factor. The customer in the above case estimated for me that his company spent at least $2,000 a year with X Airlines for his travel alone. At best they had lost his business, and at worst the business of the other 100 or so employees with similar flying habits. Under such circumstances, spending (say) $500 to effect a recovery would not have been a bad investment, but the lack of this awareness cost the company dear.

Similar things happen everywhere. Most companies have realized that it makes sense to give their customers something to try to compensate for problems, but often that compensation is inadequate. Taking a cold financial view, this may sometimes be a valid response. The film processing laboratory that loses the holiday snaps of someone who processes one film a year can't realistically pay too much to compensate. Yet some customers may get through 20 films a year or even more, and some may always be coming back for expensive enlargements. The lab that compensates all customers with the same response – a replacement film – has no idea of service recovery. It might claim that it doesn't know enough about its customers to respond appropriately, but whose fault is that? Companies have the opportunity to get enough information to build a customer database, but they may not use it.

These examples happen to be in the 'visible' world, though the recovery part often happens (or doesn't happen) remotely, after the event. However, exactly the same principles apply to dealing with the invisible customer. As much as possible, the agent dealing with a customer needs to have a feel for the customer's value. This should help drive an instant response to turn things around.

Let's imagine a frustrated customer ringing a call centre. The product she ordered hasn't turned up. 'I'm really sorry – we had problems with our computer last week and the order was never put through. OK, what I'm going to do is make sure you get one tomorrow. I'll send it guaranteed delivery, and you won't pay a penny for it – it's on us. I'm sure it will come on time, but if there is any problem, my name's Andy and my direct line is… ' The phrasing here is significant. Firstly, the agent apologizes, and comes up with a short explanation (not an excuse – it is their fault and he accepts it). He gives simple facts to put it into context. The agent then says 'What *I'm* going to do', not 'I'll have to ask my supervisor' or 'I'm not allowed'. He has shown that he is a trusted person who can make something happen, and turned this into a personal contact. He has initiated a generous compensation – getting the product free. What's more, when it arrives, there will be some sort of bonus freebie to put the icing on the cake – and because the customer's trust will have been weakened by the error, he has given her a route to chase up the problem in the unlikely event that anything else goes wrong.

As service recovery is very much a person-to-person activity, it's hard to imagine at first that the same thing could work on an online basis, but in fact it can – and there is a very real opportunity for differentiation, as few Web sites have yet discovered the art of service recovery. Let's take the example of the Amazon bookshop, not because there is necessarily anything wrong with their service recovery, but merely to show how it could happen. Books on Amazon are shown as being available in a certain timescale (eg two to three days), and the customer's expectation is that the time limit will be met. Let's imagine that, for whatever reason, a book labelled this way turns out not to be available on time. The system is capable of monitoring this. Amazon's computer knows when the book is ordered, its predicted availability time and when it is dispatched. It would be quite simple, if the book still hasn't been sent out two days after the expected delivery time, to send an apologetic personal e-mail. If it still hasn't been sent in twice the expected time, award the recipient an Amazon gift voucher to the value of the book. This is easily automated recovery that would set the e-store ahead of its competitors.

Some online recovery isn't so easy. Say the book arrives damaged or is lost in transit. In that case, you are back to an agent-handled recovery, with the advantage that the contact is liable to be by e-mail, and so doesn't require as much discretion from the agent. However, it certainly does still require a good eye to customer value when compensating if the customer isn't to defect to one of the many online competitors.

Speaking the glow

As we have already discovered, a major part of the impression you give to customers comes from non-verbal clues. On the phone, this is reduced to voice tone. If possible, agents should be given the chance to listen to tapes of their work. A combination of factors is needed to give the right impression. The more of these ways of coming across that appear in the tone, the better:

- Friendly – sounding approachable and easy to talk to.
- Interested – when customers are discussing their problems or requirements, your tone and responses show whether or not you find what they are saying interesting. React regularly with positive-sounding encouragement. Avoid 'bored', an easy tone to put across, at all costs.

- Unhurried – it doesn't matter if you have a quota of calls to get through, sounding rushed is going to destroy any glow. Being patient and unhurried (not the same as slow) is essential. Keep the conversation going, but don't rush it.
- Personal – treat the customer as an individual, not a number or just another call in your list of 200. Think how you would speak to a social contact – not a close friend, but someone you want to know better.

If it appears challenging to combine all these attributes in a simple telephone conversation, bear in mind that, however you speak, you will be placed somewhere on a spectrum in each of these areas. It's not that you switch on friendliness, just that you move towards the friendly end of the friendly-to-unfriendly spectrum.

As part of what you are trying to achieve is the effect of being in conversation with a real person, there are few things that have a more devastating effect on the glow in a telephone call than the background noise of a busy call centre. Hearing fragments of other conversations going on in the background puts your session firmly into the frame of being a mechanical production-line process. It is absolutely essential if you are to achieve a glow that there is good enough sound insulation in the call centre to make it sound as if this is a one-off, individual conversation.

What remains is the content. Scripts are deadly in this context. To give the glow, the content has to sound natural and unforced. Very few people can read a script as if they are speaking naturally. Yet the script is there for a purpose – to ensure that the agent covers the appropriate information. Consider the compromise adopted by most good public speakers. Reading a speech word for word sounds just as false as in conversation. Many speakers may start from a detailed script, but then condense their prompts into a few keywords. This means that the desired content is covered, but the exact wording comes out naturally and fresh.

Horror story

Word for word

A call centre manager recalls one of the problems with using scripts.

When I was at WCJ, I worked with a woman called Lisa, who had the same job as me in training people to give good customer service on the phone. Part of the job, as you can imagine, is getting people to be entirely natural and relaxed whilst at the same time adhering to the script created for each call. The script, as in theatre, is a combination of lines to be spoken and stage directions to guide the operator through the call.

One of Lisa's new hires – let's call her Rebecca – was showing almost crippling nervousness, but Lisa persevered with the training until at last she thought Rebecca was ready to try a live call. Lisa was relieved to hear Rebecca go through the whole call without a major slip up, though still with a shaky voice and trembling manner. All was well, until she came to the end: 'Well, Mr Farmer, we'll have the information off to you within 24 hours,' she read, and then, finally, tragically, the ultimate clash of structured script and natural communication: 'Thank respondent and close,' she said.

In the call centre, to provide a similar effect to the good public speaker's unforced delivery, it would help to have both full scripts and keyword prompts. The agents should be taken through the full scripts, but then use the keyword prompts in their conversations. How those keywords are presented depends on your requirements. In the example below there are both linear and mapped keywords. If you are prepared to take the time to produce them and give the agents familiarity with them, mapped keywords are better, as it is easier to jump around a diagram like this, which better matches the non-linear nature of most conversations. If the agents have some basic training in mapping (very useful for taking notes when on the phone), they can draw their own maps, which are easier to take in when using them live.

Script

Good morning/afternoon, my name is X from the BigCo Corporation. I'm calling you in response to your request for more information about our air conditioning products. Could I get a little more information about your requirements?

- How many rooms will you need to provide air conditioning for?
- Can we take each of those rooms one at a time?
  - What would you call the first one?
  - Roughly how big is the room?
  - Can you give me an idea of the number and size of windows?
  - How many people typically occupy the room?...

Linear keywords

Good morning/afternoon
X from BigCo
Asked info re aircon
More on requirements?
Number rooms?
One at time...
First called?
First size?
First windows?
First occupation?

Keyword map

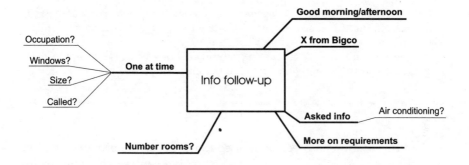

Figure 6.1   Keyword Map

The other contribution content can make to the glow is in the non-essential parts of the conversation. A social conversation might have a principal topic, but will include some small asides – about the weather, the person's health and so on. Putting such elements into a call centre conversation will lengthen the call, but will also contribute to the glow, provided they don't dominate the conversation and provided the agent sounds as if he or she is genuinely interested in the response. If dealing with existing customers, an aside might be simply to ask what they think of the product. If your systems allow the agent to know that he or she has dealt personally with a customer before (see Chapter 9), it is very effective to say 'Nice to speak to you again' or 'Yes, I spoke to you last month about that' or 'I remember us speaking late last year.' Any such social conversation, however, should be left to the natural phrasing of the agent – scripting it can be disastrous.

Horror story

Programmed chat

If there is any need to be convinced that scripts don't always work well, and that any social aspect of the call should not be scripted, here is an example where a script unwisely included the personal touch.

I recently had a call from one of the businesses that regularly ring up on the popular scam of asking for advertising in a calendar or book that supposedly supports local children's charities. 'Well, you sound really full of beans,' said the agent. 'What's your secret?' I was so taken aback, I couldn't reply. I patently didn't sound full of beans. The agent ploughed on. 'You must have had a good weekend!' In fact I had spent most of the last two nights up with a sick child. 'No,' was my short reply – before I hung up on him.

It's hard to know where to start in analysing the flaws in this performance. It was inane, insensitive and guaranteed to minimize response.

Much of this section has been addressed to the needs of outbound call centres, where scripts are more rigid, but incoming centres also tend to use greeting and diagnosis scripts, which would merit the same translation into keywords and maps. Whatever the role of the call centre, the aim is to produce a natural, friendly conversation that achieves the desired result in an appropriate time and leaves customers feeling that they have been speaking to a warm person who really cares about their requirements.

Electronic glow

Producing a feeling of individual, warm attention when you are communicating by e-mail is quite a challenge, but it is possible. For most larger companies it is impractical to handle all e-mail using individually typed letters. Templates have to be employed as a matter of course. In such circumstances, make sure that there is considerable opportunity for personalization in the template – not just the name of the sender and the agent (e-mails from individuals are the only ones that can really give the glow), but small snippets of information as well. This has to be handled carefully to avoid the old-fashioned personalized mass-mailing effect. Consider these three approaches, the first a standard letter, the second a traditional mass mailing and the third going for the glow.

Standard letter

Valued customer,

Thank you for using BigCo products in the past. We are coming up to Christmas and it's time to think of your Holiday image. Will you be sending the same old cards, or would you like to stand out from the crowd with our striking personalized gifts?

Happy Holidays,
From the BigCo Customer Service Team

Traditional mass mailing

Dear **Mr Brian Clegg,**

Thank you for using BigCo products at **Creativity Unleashed Limited**. We are coming up to Christmas and it's time to think of the Holiday image of **Creativity Unleashed Limited**. Will you be sending the same old cards, or would you like to stand out from the crowd with our striking personalized gifts from **Mr Brian Clegg** and everyone at **Creativity Unleashed Limited**?

Happy Holidays, **Mr Brian Clegg,**
Dan Sturton (Chief Executive, BigCo Corporation)

Selective personalization

Dear Brian,

Thanks for using BigCo products in the past. We are coming up to Christmas and it's time to think of your seasonal image. Last year you

> bought some of our deluxe cards. You might like to have a selection
> from the same range, or alternatively we have found that business con-
> sultancies like yours find our calendar coasters work well (these could
> be personalized with the Creativity Unleashed logo).
>
> All the best for Christmas and the New Year,
> Suzie Smith (Creativity Unleashed Limited sales contact)

Note what is happening in these examples. The first says nothing special; it
is impersonal – it is even signed by a team. The second format, especially
with the tailored fields highlighted, smacks of the terrible 'You, yes you,
Mr Brian Clegg of **Your House, Your Street**, have been specially selected
from everyone in **Yourtown**, to receive...' sort of mailings that gave certain
companies a bad name in the 1980s. Not only does the highlighting of the
fields seem artificial, but this sort of mailing patronizes the customer. There
is an unsuccessful attempt at making it more personal by putting a real person's name at the bottom, but the fact is a customer would never normally
deal with the chief executive, so he is not the right person to sign.

Compare these with the final version. The first difference is the use of
variants on the data. The contact is addressed by his first name. The company is referred to as both 'Creativity Unleashed Limited' and 'Creativity
Unleashed' depending on the format that fits the context best. The message
has been localized. The term 'Holiday' to refer to the Christmas season is
alien to a European audience, so 'seasonal' has been substituted. There is a
reference to past purchases – the writer seems to know the customer. And
there is a specific recommendation based on the knowledge of the sort of
business that is involved. The signature is that of the individual the customer
usually deals with. Even though this e-mail could have been generated totally
automatically, it has a much more personal feel – it has the glow.

Another trap to avoid in giving the glow in an e-mail is to avoid excessive
officialese and jargon. It is quite possible to make the same message feel
like a note from a friend or a directive from a council sub-committee. This is
an e-mail to a non-technical purchasing executive.

'Council' version

> Dear Mr Clegg,
>
> As a result of assessing our customers' inventory, we believe that you
> have or will be finding yourself in an ongoing sub-optimal power situation

with respect to PC CPUs. While the average clock speed of your Pentium IIIs is adequate according to the WinMark benchmark, it has been found that a minimum of 1Mb cache is essential when employing AGP and USB on the same bus architecture. It is therefore recommended that you consider deploying a motherboard upgrade on a biannual cycle, with effect from 23rd inst.

Friendly version

Dear Brian,
We've checked your PCs and think some are underpowered. Although most are fast enough, the graphics and facilities for connection to other hardware are overloading the system. We recommend upgrading every 2 years, starting on the 23rd September.

The improvement is immense. The second version starts in a friendly way. (Note, by the way, that I am not suggesting that all customers should be addressed by their first name. Some will prefer to be 'Mr Clegg'. The agent should find out how the customer prefers to be addressed.) The agent has also overcome the urge to use many words where one will do. Instead of an 'ongoing sub-optimal power situation', the PCs are simply 'underpowered'. There is no attempt to dazzle with science. Instead of using technical terms for the components, the second e-mail describes their function. Another major difference is the move from passive to active voice. 'We recommend' is preferable to 'it is therefore recommended', and also assigns responsibility for the recommendation. The passive statement, 'it has been found that', is redundant. Note the disappearance of the confusing 'biannual' in the final sentence. If there is any doubt about meaning, rephrase in simple English to abolish the ambiguity.

Good news story

Pandora's Box

Pandora's Gifts is a typical gift shop in Lechlade, a small British market town. Such shops usually struggle to make ends meet, yet this one has found that it can give the glow to its customers over the Net.

It sells British gifts and the popular Ty beanbag collector toys to customers worldwide, and sells many US products back to the US. It achieves this by making it obvious that it cares. The Pandora Web site with its update newsletters gives the impression of the little local shop that knows its stuff – but you don't have to be in Lechlade to use it.

Pandora's Gifts has a good measure of the glow. It receives frequent letters and e-mails from customers, and even gifts that its customers feel the Pandora people would like. The proprietor admits that dealing with this remote relationship can be quite a burden – but it's worth it, because it makes Pandora's Gifts into somewhere you deal with a friend, rather than an impersonal shop or Web site. There's nothing magic or hi-tech here. In fact the site doesn't look anything special – but the way the shop responds to its customers makes a lot of difference.

In the Pandora's Box story we see something beyond even the solutions recommended above. Here the letters feel personal and individual because they are. They are written by the staff of the shop, who feel they actually know many of the correspondents even though they have never met. This doesn't mean that they don't make use of stock phrases, or perhaps write one letter and then tailor it slightly for subsequent recipients, but there is always a genuinely personal touch. Why not take a similar approach?

It's easy to say that this is fine for a small shop, but not appropriate for a large company. You may believe you have too many contacts for it to be possible to work this way. However, if each agent handles a small percentage of the customer base, it is quite possible to give the 'small company feel' to communications. If you have too many customers for this approach, why not take your top 10 per cent of customers (or 5 or 20 or 50 – however many you are comfortable with handling this way) and divide them up between your agents? That way, at least your most important contacts will get a truly personal touch.

There are two points about this suggestion. The first is that you may not actually be able to identify your top 10 per cent of customers. This is not an acceptable position. When your agents pop information about the customer (see Chapter 9), they should be told that customer's importance to the company. It might be in the form of lifetime value (preferably) or ranking, but there should be some feel. If your systems can't cope with this, it's time to change them. Small companies know exactly what their customers are worth to them, and respond accordingly. You should be able to do the same.

The second point is the risk involved. You are putting the company's relationship with major customers into the hands of agents. Can you trust them to get it right? For that matter, can you trust agents with knowing the value a particular customer has to the company? This element of trust is key to getting the best out of your agents and to giving superb customer service. We will return to it in later chapters. For the moment, it is enough to note that trust will be necessary if you are really going to give agents the chance to give customers a glow.

Community spirit

It has been said of the World Wide Web that three factors mark a Web site with the glow – content, commerce and community. It is likely, as penetration of the Internet grows, and as it becomes available through a wider set of vehicles from TV sets to mobile phones, that the last 'C', community, will become even more important than it is today. What we are already seeing, which will be much stronger in a few years' time, is the opportunity to provide a sense of community to your customers.

It might start with a discussion forum hosted on your site. This might seem an opportunity for dissatisfied customers to criticize you visibly, but having the glow isn't the same as doing a whitewash job. When things go wrong, you want people to know about it – and to know what a superb effort you've made in fixing it. Such forums shouldn't be policed by members of your company (except to remove obscene or illegal entries), but it is important that you have some senior people in the company who are prepared to contribute. You often see a discussion forum with a string of moans about a company, but no response from the company itself. A similar thing happens on consumer TV shows, where companies can be vilified for ignoring their customers. It is much better if a senior spokesperson can say, 'We hear you', and shortly afterwards, 'This is what we are doing about it.'

Increasingly, as technology in this area matures, if you encourage (and practically support) a sense of community amongst your customers, you will find that they become a powerful, unpaid resource working in your favour. Customers will share experiences of your products and services, encouraging others to try out a new offering. Customers will help one other with support issues, freeing up the time of paid support staff. There's an opportunity here, if companies are prepared to grasp it.

Feel the glow

It's perhaps my fault in choosing an image like 'the glow', but there's a real danger of dismissing the subject of this chapter as waffly, airy-fairy nonsense. Taking this attitude is a mistake.

Studies of decision-making show that we all put a huge weight on the gut feel and relatively little on quantitative factors. We are much more likely to make a purchasing decision because 'it feels right' (and then use after-the-event rationalization to fit numbers to the decision) than to be guided by pure numbers. This is why companies that are dominated by their accountants rarely soar. They may plod along safely, but they aren't going to be high flyers.

It's arguable that one of the reasons we need to concentrate so much on the glow when dealing with the invisible customer is that we've got at least 10 years' worth of work to undo. The 1990s saw the explosive growth of technology that had the effect of isolating us from our customers. It's ironic that today's technology has to focus on undoing the effects of that earlier wave of technology. What a store clerk could do easily 200 years ago, we need to be able to do today, supported by the technology that can bring the individual touch back to the invisible customer relationship. We'll see more of this in Chapter 9, when we look at who the customer is, and personalization. But it's important to remember that, however good your systems, they won't give the glow – it's only people caring about other people who can.

If the customers who are going to buy your products and services feel that you don't care about them, it will influence their decision as to whether or not to use you in the future, no matter how cheap or technically advanced your product is. It might not prevent a particular purchase from going through, but it will certainly damage your long-term relationship with customers. And you want those long-term relationships, because it is a lot harder to get new business from unknown sources than from existing customers. Getting across to customers that you care and having a good working relationship with them is what the glow is all about. In the end, customer relationships are not about CRM systems and throughput metrics and ACDs – they are about people and getting the glow.

7

Long-distance selling

While mail order has been around a long time, using the phone and particularly the Web for selling is a relatively new skill. Often the lessons of many years of mail order experience are ignored to the company's cost. This chapter looks both at the lessons from elsewhere and at the very new opportunities and threats of the telephone and online environment.

What does the customer want?

Selling is a mixture of giving customers things they want and giving them things they never realized they wanted. It doesn't matter what the vehicle is, this is bound to be true. However, dealing with the invisible sales customer is quite different from the experience in a conventional store. In some ways phone shopping or Web shopping is better; in others it is worse. The important thing is to play to the strengths of the medium rather than trying to make it something it isn't.

For much of this chapter we will be using books as an example of selling goods this way. There is nothing special about books in this regard, but bookselling is one of the most mature markets on the Web, and the Web is the main focus of this chapter. If your concern is handling customer service in a call centre, you may not see selling as having much to do with you. It's still worth thinking about the implications, though. The call centre is tending to become a universal communication hub for the company, and knowledge of your products and how they are and could be sold should be part of every employee's experience.

The mail-order experience

Mail-order catalogues go back a long way, to a time when travel was not easy and most goods were delivered to the home. The mail-order vendors have stayed in business by learning about their customers, something the other media need to consider more. Specifically, mail order uses a number of techniques.

The first is the recognition of the loneliness of the long-distance shopper. Many catalogue companies have local representatives, paid a small amount of commission to provide a friendly local face for the company. This local-agent function is dying out to some degree, as one of its original purposes was to enable payment in the days when cheques and credit cards were uncommon. However, the local agent is a positive asset, and one that those dealing with many invisible customers should consider. Do you have a phone number that customers can ring if things are going wrong? If you are operating worldwide on the Web, do you have local representatives, per-haps supplied by other companies? If you also have retail outlets, can cus-tomers get support from those outlets if they are having trouble?

Another speciality of the mail-order companies is proactive selling. They don't wait for you to ask for another catalogue; they send you one. There are frequent promotions and competitions to keep customer interest. The better online sales companies have a similar approach. Recognizing the irri-tation caused by junk e-mail, they are generally a little more cautious about mailing without permission, but the possibility is there. Much more could be done in terms of competitions, though, and online companies sometimes forget that there are other media. Companies normally have a postal address for customers, because they need one when sending goods – yet they rarely make use of direct mailing about special promotions, which is something mail order always does. Similarly, the big mail-order companies sometimes use TV or newspaper advertising in a major campaign. Online or telephone-selling companies shouldn't forget the 'old' media in their campaigns.

The final tool of the mail-order company is the catalogue itself. It is a fat, attractive reminder of the products the company has on offer. It is some-thing to sit and browse through over a cup of coffee. It's often big enough to call attention to itself. Telephone and Web retailers may not have a printed catalogue, but it might be worth considering a mini-catalogue now and again to promote high-profit lines.

Subset disasters

The early days of retail on the Web were generally very poor in terms of sales. Quite a few companies, some of them very big names, set up a trial e-commerce site, found they got little response and gave up. The problem here is indicated by the word 'trial'. The companies put a small subset of their product range on a Web site. This approach overlooked the fundamental nature of both shopping and the Web.

What the companies should have asked themselves is, if they were trying out a new store in a large city, would they only stock that store with a small subset of their usual range? It's unlikely – it would be a flop. Why, then, did they expect anything different on the Web? There are significant differences between shopping on the Web and in the high street. In a conventional store it is easy to wander around and browse through the stock. That isn't so easy to do online. What an online shop can do well, though – in fact better than a conventional shop – is let you search quickly through a huge catalogue. The early adopters got it upside down. They shouldn't have offered a subset of the products of a conventional store, but a bigger range of products.

Compare the disastrous early attempts by some retailers, carrying a couple of hundred 'best seller' products, with the approach of Amazon.com, the doyen of online retailers. A typical bookshop might have between 10,000 and 40,000 books on the shelf. According to their literature, Amazon have 'the world's biggest selection of products', not a tiny subset. Even their UK subsidiary Amazon.co.uk 'stocks' around 1.2 million books, while the US parent has around twice that. How can Amazon afford such an immense stock? Of course, they don't. They rely on the fact that Web shopping is really a matter of browsing through an online database. Why not make that the database of all books in print, rather than just the books in your warehouse? The online retailer can now be seen to be at an advantage, not a disadvantage.

This stock comparison is an uncomfortable one for conventional bookshops. After all, they have always been able to order any book in print – it isn't fair to compare their shelves with the electronic catalogue. Unfortunately, as with many retail matters, it's the subjective feel that counts. It feels as if Amazon stocks all those books. In the high-street bookstore, you have to ask the assistant, who will graciously look through the catalogue for you. It just isn't the same. Even if bookshops start to have self-service kiosks providing friendly access to the whole catalogue (something they ought to seriously consider), it will seem second-rate compared with the books on the shelves. In the end, the message is simple: don't sell subsets online.

Browsing online

Whoever called the piece of software used to look at the Web a 'browser' wasn't into online commerce (but then who was in those days?). Browsing, in the sense of wandering around a shop and fingering the merchandise, is simply not something the Web does well.

Think of buying clothes, for instance. Compare choosing a jacket from a traditional store and from the online variety. In the traditional store you pick out the rack for your size. You run your eye along the merchandise, spotting colours and some hints to the styling from the side-on view. After this, you probably pull out a few jackets, getting a better look at the material, feeling it, seeing just how each one is styled. You might choose two or three. You try each jacket on and check the results in a mirror. Only then do you part with your cash. Come to the online store and it's a much less effective experience. You might choose jackets and sizing from a menu. Then perhaps you will see a list, maybe with tiny pictures. You can click on the picture and it will be made bigger, but that's the end of the browsing experience. It's not much fun.

How do the mail order people get round this? Browsing in a physical catalogue is much simpler, as it is possible to flick through many megabytes' worth of images in a fraction of a second as you turn the pages – the visual bandwidth of a printed catalogue is greater than is practical on the Web. Some companies also provide swatches of material so you can get the look and feel of it.

It should be possible to take a similar approach with the Web. You could imagine a mail-me-a-swatch button. You could take a lesson from some of the smaller mail order companies, who use designer's line drawings of the clothes – much easier to display quickly on the Web – along with swatches. You could envisage a Web site with small patches of material down the side. Customers would flip quickly between line drawings, and then choose one, which would be displayed full screen with the selected material.

You could go further still with an online clothes rail. Most online shops don't have the concentrated view of a large number of products that a clothes rail gives, but there's no reason why this shouldn't be possible. Or imagine customers being able to download clothes modeller software from the Web site. If they see a design they might like on the site, that too would be downloaded. They add a picture of themselves and the modeller software gives a 3D picture of them wearing the design – all perfectly practical with today's technology.

Of course your business could be totally different – you might be dealing with something much less tangible – but the broad requirement is the same. Customers want to be able to get the best possible feel for your products without huge online time and costs. This might mean presenting your products in a different way, or having hybrid conventional and online, or online and downloaded presentation. The important thing is to examine a wider range of options, and be more creative, than has normally been the case up to now.

I want a green widget

Online shops are on much firmer ground when customers know exactly what they want. The powerful search facilities built into most e-commerce sites make it easy to locate a green widget or a book by Fred Smith. The trick some sites miss is the need to have both an 'easy search', which lets you type anything into a box but isn't too fussy – so searching for Fred Smith will give you books about blacksmiths as well as Fred's works – and also a detailed search, which lets you specify the search characteristics – with books this might be author, title, ISBN, publisher or subject.

The hybrid shopper

There is an in-between state. Taking the book example again, I might want a book about light or Citroën 2 CV cars or sausage manufacture. I don't know the title or the author – I don't even know if a specific book exists – but I know what I want it to be about. Neither of the conventional ways of navigating an online store is exactly right. I could look for books with 'light' or 'Citroën' or 'sausage' in the title, but there will be plenty of dross, and plenty of appropriate books that simply don't have the keyword in the title.

Alternatively, I could browse. Like the real thing, online bookshops arrange their books by category. However, the categories are very broad, and though I would come to some items I wanted this way, I would be unlikely to reach much on 'Citroën' or 'sausage'. With 'light', the chances are that the closest I would get is physics, and even then I would only see a small subset of the total books that could fit into this category.

Action station

Spot the Citroën

Go to the Amazon bookstore (www.amazon.com or www.amazon.co.uk) and try
to find books on Citroën cars. The exercise is a valuable one in understanding
how a relatively easy process in a physical shop can be much harder online.

What is needed in such circumstances is a hybrid search facility that allows
the customer to be quite specific about a subject without having a particular book in mind. Amazon has a 'search by category' facility, but this is very
limited. When I searched for my three sample categories, 'light' came up
with plenty of entries, mostly about light music, and 'Citroën' and 'sausage' were totally blank (though I did get some interesting references on
'usage'). The problem seems to be that the category search is dependent on
keywords input by the shop, and there are many specifics not covered.

Homing in on an appropriate selection could be achieved, however, and
the example of how to do it is already on the Web in the form of full word
search engines like AltaVista, which let you look up any word on any page
on the site. For instance allowing a full word search on all the text in the
articles on each book would trawl in most relevant books, because the
chances are that the subject matter you are interested in will come up somewhere. Unfortunately this would also pull in plenty of dross. At this point
you would need a negative filter, where the keywords that already exist
would come in valuable. If the customer could take the list returned and say
'not like this' (for instance, eliminating music from a 'light' search), it
would soon be possible to whittle a list down to a manageable number.

A hybrid task like this is quite possible, as long as the site designers
think through what people really want to do. It's just the same as an IVR
menu or the procedure for dealing with a caller at a call centre. It has to be
the task that the customer is trying to achieve that drives the mechanics
and the process.

Good news story

Hitting the right note

I recently sent an e-mail to UK book and music specialists Blackwell's, asking whether it was possible to buy sheet music over the Web, and also chasing up an order I had made while last in their Oxford shop. I received this mail in reply:

> Dear Mr. Clegg,
>
> Thank you for your message, which has been passed on to me by our online bookshop. By all means order music by e-mail. We do not have a Web site to browse but, to be honest, you will find me much more use than a Web site anyway!
>
> About the Harold Darke. The Mag and Nunc in A Minor seems to be out of print. I will do some digging and try to find out some definite information for you. Sorry about its getting lost.
>
> Best wishes,
>
> Peter McMullin
> Printed Music Specialist

Mr McMullin has a point. If it is possible to provide a human hybrid service, you are probably going to be more effective than anything a Web site can do. Having an e-mail address to ask an expert for advice, whether you then continue to process the order through a Web site or simply continue the transaction through e-mail, is an attractive proposal that would provide a real customer service benefit.

The quick buy

Think about the actual process of buying a product in a store or over the phone. You have made your selection, and now you want to pay for it and take it away. In the store, it is very simple. The sales assistant enters your purchases in the till (probably using a scanner). You are presented with a total and either produce the cash or use a card, which is swiped through a machine. You then sign a docket, and walk out with the product under your arm or have it delivered. On the phone you will almost certainly use a card and need to go through the two stages of giving your card details and a delivery address.

Compare these two with a typical experience of buying from a Web site. You fill in a form, which itself can be irritating, as the behaviour of forms may not be quite what you expect. The need to tab from field to field may be alien to some customers, as indeed may be the need to type. The form may be broken into several chunks, for both timing and security reasons, so between each stage of the form you have to wait for a new page to load. This can take 10 seconds or more on a slow line. Assuming the company uses a secure site for financial transactions, there may be warnings about security and the possibility of browsers not working with a secure server. This all adds to the nervousness of customers sending critical financial data across an Internet that the media indicate is rife with hackers and mad programmers, all out to get their hands on credit card details. All in all, the online buying process is not a happy one.

Compare this with the 1-Click buying process employed by the Amazon online bookshops. Having decided on the book you want to buy, you click the button on the page labelled 'Buy Now With 1-Click™ (you can always cancel it later).' That's it. You have bought it, and you don't need to be worried about sending credit card details across the Internet, because you are not required to. Not only is this approach better than the normal online buying process, it's better than the experience over the phone or in a real store.

It's easy to come up with objections to the 1-Click approach, but they can be countered. The customer does have to fill in a form in the first place to establish 1-Click settings (though the settings could alternatively be set up by fax or letter). However, unless customers only ever buy one product from you, they will benefit. It might also be objected that 1-Click is just an account by another name. It is an account, but Amazon is making use of the technology to ensure that using an account involves nothing more than a twitch of your mouse finger.

Making 1-Click work is complex from a systems viewpoint. For example, the Amazon system bundles up 1-Click purchases made over several hours into a single order to reduce shipping costs. Nevertheless, providing something similar to 1-Click is an essential if you really want buying to be easy for your customers. Anyone with repeat business should consider this very seriously. It is a customer service enhancement that requires no time from your agents – it is all handled by the technology – making it superbly cost-effective while simultaneously attractive for the invisible customer. (At the time of writing, Amazon is attempting to patent 1-Click, but the principle still applies.)

Thinking global

There's typically one big difference between selling on the Web and on the phone. Most phone selling is done in the country of your business operation. By the very nature of the Web, customers can come from anywhere in the world. This doesn't mean you have to be able to cope with anything from anywhere. However you should be aware of your main markets. For instance, any UK site is liable to pick up customers from the US and Europe. Similarly, US sites are liable to be attractive to the UK, to the whole of North, Central and South America, and to the Pacific Rim countries. Language, location and product all drive just whom you attract to your site. If you want to keep and please your customers, you must overcome the parochial viewpoint that might have been good enough for the domestic market.

Horror story

Tickets online

This example shows the problems that can arise when a company hasn't realized the implications of the 'World Wide' part of World Wide Web. This incident happened a while ago; the site in question has changed since. The customer was working in the UK at the time.

> I'm a pretty wired kind of guy; I can do stuff online. Next weekend I'm taking my girlfriend to New York, so when we decided to see a Broadway show, I knew just what to do. Stay tuned here, because this is a tale of human passions with a lesson for the Web.
>
> I went to http://newyork.sidewalk.com – and another site I can't remember – and read up a load of show reviews. We wanted to see a musical. *Chicago* and *1776* both looked good. So through Yahoo I found two good sites where I could book tickets online, http://www.ticketmaster.com and http://www.nettiks.com. It turned out that *Chicago* was sold out for the weekend, and NetTiks (part of Telecharge) didn't offer *1776*, so I could only book it through the Ticketmaster site. I started going through the motions.
>
> The date and price I wanted were available, but when it came to giving my details the site insisted on asking which US state I live in – unfortunately I wasn't in the US. I spent a lot of time trawling the site for information on whether I could purchase a ticket from outside the US, but could find none. So I looked for an e-mail contact. I found one page that said, to provide feedback, click on the 'contact' link on the left of this page. I did this, and

was returned to the same page. I called the US Ticketmaster number at international rates. On connection I had to listen to an advert that was irrelevant to me before being offered keypad choices. On making my choice I was put on hold – for too long.

At this point it was late. I gave up, with only slight wisps of smoke coming from my ears, and went to bed. I tried again the next day. I returned to the site to make sure I hadn't made a mistake somewhere. It turned out that I had – but only as far as the feedback link goes. I had clicked on the wrong 'contact' button, of which there were a number on the left-hand side. I sent a forceful but polite enquiry to which a couple of days later I have yet to receive a reply. Not much good if the show sells out. So I thought to check out how well they have integrated the site into the business. I called Ticketmaster in the UK, who gave me another UK number. They didn't know anything about the Web site, and didn't know anyone else who did. They also couldn't book me a ticket for a Broadway show as 'the link to New York won't be up for about a month'. They gave me a US number to call. This turned out to be the number for Telecharge – of NetTiks fame. No they couldn't book the show I wanted. I'd have to call Ticketmaster.

This time I hung on long enough to talk to a person. He thought that I couldn't book on the US site as I would have to have a US phone number, although he made no suggestion what to do about being asked for a US address. He could give me a US 800 number to talk to someone about it, but I can't call an 800 number from the UK. He didn't have an alternative number. He could however, book my ticket. We went through the motions until he asked me for a US telephone number. I put the phone down as politely as I could. I was enraged. How difficult can someone make it to take money off you? A check of the Theatre's Web page yielded only the Ticketmaster number. A call to another US ticket agency yielded the fact that they could only book me premium rate tickets for the show. For the tickets I wanted I had to call… Ticketmaster.

My aversion to Ticketmaster was only slightly outweighed by my desire to please my girlfriend. I finally booked through Ticketmaster, having found the number of the hotel that I would be staying at, and giving them that. Incidentally, the NetTiks site does have separate input fields depending on whether you are booking from inside or outside of the US.

On top of the booking fee Ticketmaster also charged me a 'convenience fee'. You've gotta laugh, or you'd kill someone.

The Ticketmaster example shows just how easy it is to make it difficult for a customer who is in a country with the same language, and who even wants a product that will be delivered in the Web site's native country. Getting state or zip code information from customers and providing an 800 number to call isn't bad, but it's essential to make sure that your systems don't insist on using these domestic-only vehicles.

International considerations fall into three main areas (all of which are to some extent about communication): language, offline communications and dispatch, though there will also be matters like taxation to consider.

Language

Dealing with a worldwide audience, language is bound to crop up occasionally. If you come from an English-speaking country, you are at an advantage – partly thanks to the Web, English is now secure as *the* international language – and an English-language site will usually give you the best return on a single site. However, if a sizeable percentage of your customer base is in a non-English-speaking country (especially if it is a country with strong language preferences, such as France), it is worth investing the time and effort to have a local language variant of your site.

If it is practical, consider a locally hosted (to increase access speed) and locally maintained site, which can not only use the host language, but also cover items specific to the host country's requirements, oriented to the host country's cultural inclinations. Even with an English-speaking site, if your customer base has large representations in (say) both the US and Australia, you may consider a regional site.

A final consideration on language: try, as far as possible, to avoid having items on your site that are likely to be offensive in a different language. It is impossible to monitor every word on your site in every language, but you might at least consider having a native speaker check out your site if it is widely used by a country with a different first language. Sometimes you might be helped by outsiders. I received the following e-mail about my company's site, www.cul.co.uk. The writer translated from his original French using an automatic translator, hence the rather quaint language.

> Please allow the transfer, I use a mechanical software because I very English of cannot.
>
> On the 14ème, in the porque one, I slap a search with the form returned www.cul.co.uk. Then to say to you, cul is a bad French word? It average rest-on the flesh of the rectum of anybody.
>
> Since this, cannot think you the need to want the nation French with the arrangement of creative. Thus I give to help in all fraternity, to think please for the change.
>
> Familiar the most pleasant
>
> Henri.

Apart from illustrating wonderfully the dangers of working in an unfamiliar language (or of using automatic translation), the writer was informing my company that the acronym CUL (for Creativity Unleashed Limited) has unfortunate connotations in French. This presented something of a quandary. We did not want to lose our three-letter Web site name, which is something of a prize, so we put a disclaimer on the front page of our site in French, explaining why the name is as it is.

One very specific aspect of language is units of measurement. Although there is worldwide scientific acceptance of the metric mks system of units, many countries maintain local variants. The most significant is the US, which has been much slower to accept metric measurements that the rest of the world. The most drastic recent example of this was in 1999, when a space probe crashed on Mars because the US scientists (like all scientists, working in metric units) hadn't realized that the US engineers who built the probe were still working in feet and inches. If you specify any measurements in your Web site, consider providing metric measurements as well as your local scales, as this will give the information more meaning worldwide. Conversely, if you come from a metric-oriented country and want to sell into the US, include the old weights and measures.

Although it's stretching a point to label these as language variants, remember that even your stock may have regional variants, whether it's the language in which a piece of software appears on the screen, standard paper sizes (for example, Letter in the US, A4 anywhere in Europe), the voltage, the TV standard, the DVD region... and so on.

Offline communications

Sometimes you can conduct your entire business online. This is particularly true when selling downloadable software or information. More often, though, there is a need for communication away from the Web site, which might involve telephone calls, faxes or postal connections.

If you need to list telephone and fax numbers, use the international format: for example, the UK number 01777-888-9999 would be listed as +44-1777-888-9999, while the US number (222)-333-4444 would become +1-222-333-4444. The + sign indicates 'Put the international prefix here, or (typically) 0 if you are internal to the country', and may need to be explained to your customers.

A particular consideration is toll-free numbers (800 in the US, 0800 in the UK). These numbers are not generally usable outside the host country. By all means list a toll-free number, but list a conventional one too for callers from outside the country. If you have a reasonable number of clients in a particular country, consider listing a number in that country, or pay the country's telecommunications operator to provide an apparently domestic number that in fact connects to your call centre.

Unlike the Web, fax and e-mail, time is an important matter with phone calls. Unless your lines are available 24 hours a day, 7 days a week, it is worth specifying the availability, and the time zone it applies to. Don't just use a local term (for example, Eastern Standard Time or British Summer Time); make it clear how that fits with the global time standard, and include both 12- and 24-hour clocks. For example, you might say, 'Phone lines available 8 am to 6 pm (08:00 to 18:00) Eastern Standard Time (GMT + 5 hours).'

If you expect postal communications, remember to specify your address in a way that can be used by your correspondents. This particularly needs to be thought out if you are dealing with customers using a different alphabet. For instance, if your company is based in Belarus, you might want to include your address in Cyrillic even on an English-language site. But you can't assume that your customers will have Cyrillic fonts on their computers, so you would have to show the address as a graphic.

You also need to consider what address details you require from customers. As we've already seen in the Ticketmaster example, it is no good using a form where customers have to choose a US state, if some of them live outside the US. Similarly, don't force a particular format for a phone number or zip code (remember to give this the more generally recognized title of 'postal code'). Another one to watch out for is customer location. Nick Gassman, who provided the Ticketmaster example, points out that some sites ask you to select whether you are 'US' or 'overseas'. However, very few people are 'overseas' when they are using a Web browser: they are at home and, if they aren't in the US, it's the US that is overseas to them. Using less locationist language (eg asking people to select a continent, or just 'US' and 'rest of world') would be more acceptable.

Dispatch

If you are selling a physical item, you need to get the goods to the customer. Having charges that reflect different shipping rates to any individual country will result in a very complex structure. Try instead to keep your shipping structure down to a maximum of three or four levels with very clear distinctions.

Cold e-mails – learning from junk

Junk e-mails can be the bane of an online customer's life. Particularly if customers use one of the free e-mail services like Hotmail, they will receive a hundred or more junk messages a week. To cope with this very real information overload, cold selling e-mails are increasingly being filtered out, either automatically using mail screening software or by eye. Typical cold selling e-mails tend to have a similar look and feel. In a moment we will examine the contents of some of them to see where they go wrong. In most cases, it is possible to tell they are trying to sell something before even reading the title.

The first giveaway is the 'from' information. Unwanted e-mail often comes from mailers with strange nonsense names. One of the e-mails, on which the examples below are based, was from slkdafj@dns.bigco.it (I lied about the 'bigco' bit). Few normal correspondents have addresses like this. Another giveaway is the 'to' list, which very commonly includes a large number of addresses, all from the same ISP, as recipient. Either of these signs immediately makes a mail seem suspicious. If you are trying to cold sell, make sure that your mail comes from a clear name (fred@bigco.com or, just possibly, sales@bigco.com, though fred will go down better), and that the 'to' item contains only the address of the specific recipient.

Here are three examples, very like real junk e-mails I have received in recent days:

Cold sell 1

We created this just for you!

A VACATION JUST FOR YOU!

TO THE MOST EXOTIC PLACE ON EARTH...FLORIDA!
SPECIAL ONLINE PROMOTIONAL VACATION PACKAGE IS BROUGHT TO YOU FOR A LIMITED TIME ONLY, SO DON'T WAIT! VISIT OUR WEBSITE NOW FOR MORE INFORMATION ON PRICE AND PACKAGE INFO.

(sorry, offer not available to travel agents for resale)

OFFER NOW AVAILABLE WORLD WIDE!!!

For Full Details go to: http://9876543210/ab2/abcd9/trip.html

For removal from our mailing list please go to:
http://9876543210/ab2/abcd9/removepage.html

In this example, the title immediately puts you on edge. It uses an exclamation mark and has a big-brotherly feel. It doesn't have any of the characteristics of an e-mail from another human being. Most of the actual text is in capitals, the e-mail equivalent of shouting. The content has an unwarranted familiarity. How could this vacation be created 'just for me'? The three exclamation marks after 'WORLD WIDE' are all too common. Repeated exclamation marks are used so frequently in junk mail that it is one of the ways an e-mail junk filter weeds out the rubbish. (It is worth studying some commercially available filters in e-mail packages to see just what they do use to categorize junk.) Notice also the form of the Web address. Reputable companies will have a brand-name address – it is always suspicious when a company hides behind a number. Finally, there is no signature. It is not an e-mail; it's a notice or an advertisement – one that you didn't want to receive.

Cold sell 2

Hi, Do you want Financial and Time Freedom within 2–3 years?

Do you have a work ethic above the norm?
Do you have a white hot burning desire to be successful and wealthy?
Do you know where you are headed in life?
If you can honestly answer yes, keep reading!
I don't want to waste your time or mine. This is NOT a program for everybody. Only the tough and determined will make it. If you are looking for a 'get rich on $30 program' then delete this message. You won't find that here. If you know what your goals are and are looking for a way to take you there that won't take half of your lifetime call me!

I'm short on time, but ready to listen if you fit the description above. I'm happy to help you but you must call me first. Listen to my message, and if you like what you hear, leave your name and number, and I'll call you back as soon as I can. Your age or debt load is not important to me, only the willingness to fulfill your potential.

24 hour recording
Toll Free 800-123-456
ext. 7890

NOT MLM OR FRANCHISE

'Smart is when you believe only half of what you hear.
Brilliant is when you know which half to believe.'
Anonymous

This is a rather more sophisticated attempt at cold selling than the first example. There has been an attempt to make the subject look a little bit more personal with that opening 'Hi.' Without it, the sender presumably thought, this would sound horribly like a get-rich-quick scheme, the sort that we are usually assured isn't pyramid selling – either because it really is pyramid selling, but they're calling it something different, or because it involves ridiculous effort to earn anything sizeable ('You can make $10,000 a month stuffing envelopes'). Unfortunately, it still does sound like such a scheme. The indications become stronger as we get into the body of the mail. There's an evangelistic fervour about the repeated 'Do you' sentences.

It's not all bad. Although it would have made more sense if it had come from a real person, with a real name at the bottom, the use of a quote as a tag is something commonly used in e-mail signatures, so that gives it a slight touch of honesty, as do the personal remarks in the mid-section. There are, however, three remaining failures. First, it's not signed. Second, the means of getting in touch is a toll free 800 number, which can only be dialled from the US, so sending it to an e-mail address in the UK is point-less. Finally, there's the disclaimer about it not being MLM (pyramid sell-ing) or franchise. That the sender felt it necessary to say this means that the e-mail feels as though it *is* about one of these topics. The best way to avoid this misapprehension is to phrase the mail in the first place so it's clear that this isn't your subject.

Cold sell 3

SPAINSH CEDAR CIGAR HUMIDORS !

*There is no need to respond to the above e-mail address to be removed. **
This is a 1 time mailing.

****
* AUTHENTIC SPANISH CEDAR CIGAR HUMIDORS !! *
****

Click Here or Visit to View These Exquisite Pieces !
Http://9876543210/xy/humidor

---

*We Have Recently Acquired a Small Bundle of Beautifully
Hand-Crafted Top Quality Cigar Humidors !*

*Unlike most humidors on the market today that are fabricated with MDS, (a
type of compressed fiberboard) which reduces the life of your box, These 'one of a
kind' humidors are Constructed of Solid Hardwood, fully lined with Authentic
Spanish Cedar & are designed to preserve the taste, aroma, & freshness of your
cigars !*

****
*
* Why Pay Hundreds of $ For a Humidor When This
*
* Exquisite Humidor Carries all the Quality,
*
* Durability, & Fine Craftsmanship of Pricier Boxes !
*
****

*All Humidors Come Complete With Humidification unit,
Care Instructions, Limited Life Time Warranty, &*

~A 30 Day Unconditional Money Back Guarantee !!

****
* Only $98.00 *
****

Respond Within 72 Hours and Receive Your Free Bonus Gift !

*YOU WILL NOT FIND A BETTER PRICE ON WORKMANSHIP OF THIS
QUALITY GUARANTEED !!*

These Select Humidors are a Must See !

****
* Click Here to View These Unique Pieces ! *
* http://9876543210/xy/humidor   *

****

This is a classic disaster of a junk mail apart from one saving grace. Most junk e-mails are selling things few people want to buy. This one is for an actual product that might have some value. As it happens, it has no value to me, because I don't smoke, but someone out there probably does want a good humidor. It's a shame, though, that the whole thing starts off badly by misspelling 'Spanish'.

We then get on to a popular feature of junk mail, the star box. This long (overlong) mail has four sections boxed by stars. Star boxing is another of the traits that junk mail filters tend to look for. The technique has a respectable history. Star boxes were used in computer code to make comments stand out, and in the text-only world of basic e-mail they make a sort of sense. However, not only are they a trade mark of junk mails, star boxes simply don't work any more. Many e-mail packages display the output in proportional fonts, and will render the carefully rectangular boxes into a distracting mess. It's arguable that you should either go for straight text, with just (very sparsely used) single lines of characters as separators, or use formatted mail like HTML mail, of which more in the next section.

There are enough exclamation marks in this mail to trip the junk filter, and the space inserted between the word and the '!' in each case makes the layout look sloppy. That's a minor matter compared with the use, once again, of a number-based Web site, with its implication that the sender has something to hide. Apart from that, there is an excess of capital letters, and it goes on with the superlatives so long that it feels false. This last criticism may be a regional problem. A greater level of hyperbole is probably more acceptable in some world markets than in the European one, but the mail should not have been sent to a European address.

Cold e-mails – getting it right

Even the low-grade e-mails above will get some sales, so it might seem there's an argument that it doesn't really matter about getting cold e-mails right. Provided you can send them out to enough people – and that's the joy of e-mail, it's as cost-effective to mail a million as one – you will get returns. As is often the case with bad customer service, however, this is a dangerously short-sighted view.

In simple economic terms it makes sense to get it right, because a well-structured cold e-mail campaign will result in a much higher return rate. However, this extra revenue is as nothing compared with the loss of goodwill that bad cold e-mails generate. The level of irritation should not be underestimated – they really are disliked. The following tips will help in the design of your cold e-mails.

Quick tips

Cold e-mails

- Manage your lists well. In one day recently I received seven different copies of the same e-mail advertising an online casino. I had had maybe a dozen in the previous week. The mails came from two different originating addresses, but the message was the same. Anyone receiving multiple copies gets irritated – make sure that your lists are kept tight.
- Aim for focus. If there is any way you can target your e-mail, do so. Don't broadcast to an unstructured mailing list, narrowcast to a list of people with specific interests or business activities.
- Personalize. Part of the irritation of much cold e-mail is its mechanical nature.
- Find a hook. If you can make it obvious that your e-mail is sent as a result of something you found out about the person or the company, there is a much better chance of being taken seriously. I don't ignore e-mails that start, 'I noticed in one of the books you wrote… ' Of course this means manual intervention in each mail, but it is worth it to maximize results.
- Make it look good. Companies spend millions on the look of their advertising, but many cold e-mails look scruffy. Consider HTML mail (see below).
- Give them the chance to say 'no' to any more. While many customers don't trust 'remove' options (they are sometimes used to check whether mail accounts are still alive), it is still a good idea to provide one.

Any cold e-mail will irritate some customers – but by taking the effort to minimize the irritation and increase the chances that the mail will be genuinely useful to the recipient, it is possible to make the cold e-mail a more practical business tool.

One particular consideration in producing a cold e-mail is whether or not to use HTML mail. Traditionally e-mails were pure text with no formatting. The best you could do was lay them out with spaces and characters like stars to make boxes. As discussed above, this looks amateurish, is now widely associated with the worst end of junk e-mail and doesn't even work if the mail software uses a proportional font, where the spacing of different letters varies, throwing the shape of the box out.

A very attractive alternative is to use HTML mail. This uses the same layout language as Web pages to provide formatting information. You can use different fonts, font sizes and colours. There are tables and bullet points. You can include pictures and clickable links in the text. Using HTML mail, your cold e-mail can look as professional and businesslike as any Web site, or as a quality mailer that arrives in the conventional post. There is, however, a catch.

HTML mail was supported by the major e-mail packages from around 1998. There is still plenty of e-mail software in use that does not support HTML mail. If you are lucky, the recipient will just see the basic text in the message, though without all your beautiful formatting. If you are unlucky, the recipient will also see all the tags – the layout information that tells HTML what to do with the text – making it virtually unreadable.

Making the HTML decision is a difficult call. If your typical customers are home users, games players or early adopters, you are safe using HTML. If they are corporate business users, it is significantly less likely they can make use of the formatting. As cold e-mailing tends to be more to a domestic market, the chances are that it is worth going for HTML e-mail. Certainly include an option to have any future mailings sent text only, but make use of the attractive appearance of a well-designed HTML page to give your cold e-mails the professional edge.

Speaking on the phone

Much has been written about telephone sales, so in this section, and also the following one on outbound call centres, I will restrict consideration to the very specific aspects of enhancing service to the invisible customer. In earlier chapters we looked at toll free numbers and the use of IVR. Other telephone technology will be considered later in the book. But what happens when the customer speaks to the agent?

To make the buying experience effective, probably the main consideration is that customers are not walking catalogues. By all means ask for a product reference, but it should be possible to identify the product without anything more than a human-style description. Similarly, don't expect repeat customers to know their customer reference. If they are ringing about a sale that has already been initiated, don't expect them to know an invoice number. They know who they are and what they have ordered – that ought to be good enough.

When it comes to payment, give repeat customers the opportunity to use a previously recorded credit card number and delivery details. That way you can simulate the 1-Click approach that Amazon has triumphed with on the Web. Make it as simple as possible to get that order completed.

A final consideration is one of positive attitude and support. It isn't enough to sound pleased to be dealing with the customer (although that is necessary). With many products, particularly hi-tech products, there should be no condescension. A lot of customers feel they don't really know enough about technology, so will be defensive when ordering a technical product. Help make this an easy experience.

The support part of this consideration is important. If the customer, for instance, is buying a PC peripheral that requires a separate cable, it should-n't be left to him or her to think of it. When I was working most of the time as an IT journalist, I bought hardware over the phone regularly, and never once was I asked if I had the appropriate cable for the product. Ask. Be prepared to diagnose the right sort of cable, too. A similar approach should be taken with consumables. Staying in the IT field, many customers are now buying colour printers to print photographs. Why not ask if they need appropriate consumables (photographic paper) when they buy the printer? It helps customers, who aren't frustrated when unable to use the new product without a second order, and it helps your company by adding to the sale.

The cold call

Cold calls are so unwelcome that it is hard to define just what could make a good cold call. Junk e-mail may be an irritation, but at least you can handle it at a time of your own choosing, and can generally dispose of it in a fraction of a second. By contrast, cold calls always seem to come at an inopportune time. Historically, because of our socialization, most recipients of cold calls found it hard to resist being drawn into a conversation, because that's what is expected on the phone.

There is some evidence, though, of a change in social conditioning, as cold calls become a more frequent part of life. There is at least anecdotal evidence that customers are becoming less tolerant of cold calls, being prepared more often to be rude, to talk across the agent to say 'No, thank you' or simply to put the phone down. The cold call is in need of an overhaul.

Let's start by thinking what is wrong with the cold call. There is the protective lie. Customers are becoming increasingly sophisticated. They know when you start a call by saying, 'I'm not selling anything', that you are doing just that. Then there's the memory trick, when the caller may say, 'We called you a while ago and you showed an interest in...', hoping the recipient will not realize that the call never existed. Some companies also have very poor monitoring of those called. Not only will some companies call the same house several times in a month, they have even been known to call a customer who has already agreed to take the product – not encouraging for repeat business.

Too much of the traditional cold call smacks of deception or incompetence. There is a need now for more honesty and better targeting. Without a major overhaul, the cold call will become a liability. Think of what a good cold call should do. It is a news service. You are informing a potential customer of something he or she might want, but doesn't know about. Get the benefits up front as much as possible.

Phones versus Internet

As a vehicle for incoming sales calls (ie calls to the call centre), the phone has a good pedigree. Customers are generally happy about calling up to order something. The Web equivalent has something to learn here. Longer term, we can expect Internet and phone to achieve a balance. However, it is arguable that the outgoing call approach to selling is in significant danger when faced with the much more cost-effective approach of outbound e-mail sales.

Until the Internet has a wide enough penetration, there will still be the need for outbound sales calls, but the writing is on the wall. A good e-mail is easier and cheaper to send and can carry much more information. Even the traditional advantage an outbound call had, that customers are reluctant to say no to another person, seems to be changing as customers increasingly cut off outbound calls.

Delivering on the promise

A final consideration in the sales arena is completing the sale successfully. Salespeople often think that the sale is completed when the customer has signed on the dotted line. In customer-service terms, nothing could be further from the truth: the sale has only just begun at that point. Unless the customer is supported through the period between ordering and delivery – and the delivery and goods are satisfactory – the whole precarious relationship with the customer is at risk. In the conventional sales world, the best-known offenders are car salesmen, who are all attention until the sale is closed, and then provide hardly any support despite the fact that a car is a major purchase.

The bad news for the online world is that things look just as bad as in the car salesroom. Statistics from 1999 show that nearly one in 10 items ordered over the Net never arrive at their destination. In a study by Consumers International, 45 per cent of products arrived without receipt, and 25 per cent of vendors did not provide any contact details. With figures like these, it is hard to build trust in the customer base that online buying is an effective way of proceeding. The online customer process has to stretch right through to the packing and delivery process.

While customer service agents might not be responsible for the final details of the sale, they are likely to get the flak when things go wrong. It would be a very good investment of call centre or Web support time to have an understanding of the processes that lead to delivery, and an involvement in enhancing these processes. Exactly what contact information goes with the goods, for example, is of prime interest for anyone who is caring for the invisible buyer.

We've covered keeping the customer informed elsewhere (see Chapter 5), but the message is simple. The main points are good communication of what is going on, easy redress for problems, and doing what you say when you say. Many transactions fall down on the mechanics of delivery. Improving delivery will not only enhance your chances of keeping the customer for future purchases, but will also reduce your customer support costs, as you won't receive angry calls and e-mails.

8

Speed and content

This chapter is the first of two that bridge the earlier, outward-facing chapters and the later, inward-facing chapters. It looks at the essential quality measures for communication with invisible customers – speed of response and quality of content.

Response times

It would be difficult to over-stress the importance of two prime components underlying most remote customer service – speed and content. Let's take speed first, and specifically the time taken to respond to a customer's voice mail message or e-mail. There seems to be a huge misconception underlying the way many telephone and Internet-based services respond, the basis for this misconception apparently being an assumption that dealing with remote customers has more in common with postal transactions that personal ones.

If customers came into your shop and asked for some information, it wouldn't be unreasonable for them to wait. But they would be justifiably irritated if they were still waiting after a week. Yet similar waits for a response to a query by phone or from a Web site are horribly common.

Horror story

Non-interactive investor

It is often easy to interpret a lack of response as a value judgement on the customer. I use a (usually) very helpful online share portfolio service called Interactive Investor (www.iii.co.uk). Like others of its kind, it allows you to enter your share details and monitor their climbs and falls. You can even set triggers to alert you to when a share hits a particular value. Yet, as I have already mentioned, for a share-dealing newcomer, the information can be confusing. Each share carries four prices (bid, ask, open and last). For investors who simply want to know what their shares would realize, or how much a new purchase would cost, the four prices may be confusing. As there is no obvious interpretation of the price labels on the site, I sent an e-mail asking for clarification. There was no reply.

Whether or not intended, the implied message was either that my question was so stupid it wasn't worth replying to, or that as a non-paying customer I wasn't worth dealing with. It doesn't matter whether you are charging for a service or offering it free, your customers should reasonably be able to expect timely replies to queries. If you can't manage this, it's time to get out of the business.

There is a view, with which I have some sympathy, that people don't expect the same sort of response times from queries to remote services that they do face to face. At the moment it is probably acceptable to respond within 12 hours by phone, or up to two working days for an e-mail, but too often these times are not met.

They are in any case just the starting point. If you really want to be considered something special when it comes to remote customer service, you ought to be thinking of something better. Reasonable targets are responding to a voice request within two working hours and an e-mail within four. If you can't get the answer back in that timescale, you should still get a message to the customer to explain what is happening. This should be absolutely standard, so why isn't it happening?

E-mails have it relatively easy in this respect. As we have already noted (see Chapter 5), the use of an auto responder, if properly worded, can give the impression that something is happening. But even a good auto responder is no substitute for an answer. It makes holding on for those four hours (or even two days) more comfortable, but it's not as good as an instant reply.

We'll get back to you

Some voice systems divert your call to a voice mail system when loads are high. The message is something like 'Our operators are all busy with calls right now. Leave us your contact details and we'll get back to you as soon as they are free.' This approach seems a good one. Customers are not left holding on at their own expense – in fact, you take over the responsibility for phone call costs – yet a common response to this offer is to put the phone down. Why?

The answer is, sadly, bitter experience. In a surprisingly high number of cases, when customers leave contact details in this way, they are never called back. In some call centres this is because recorded messages are given low priority, so they are rarely picked up. The voice mail approach is only really acceptable if your call centre technology can register a voice mail as another customer in the queue, and provide it with call-back as soon as it is reached. Customers using voice mail expect a call within minutes, not hours and certainly not days.

When the voice mail approach fails, you have damaged the relationship with customers even more than by being slow to respond, and more than if they had not been able to get through. If customers ring a company and don't get an answer, they retain responsibility for getting through. If, on the other hand, your company promises to ring them back, it is reasonable to feel that they have handed over responsibility to you. Failure to ring back may mean that serious consequences ensue, which the customers will blame entirely on you.

What is quality content?

However good your presentation, however much you give a glow when you talk to customers, you will always be measured on how well you deliver on your promise. Good service recovery can overcome failings in this area, but only for so long. You have to get the content right.

Horror story

Getting it right

It's back to BT's heavy-usage discount scheme (see Chapter 2) for this story. That BT appears twice does not indicate they are any worse than other companies providing remote customer service, merely that more horror stories were provided by real customers, as was this one.

> Telephone Customer Service (outsourced, I think, not BT directly – not quite sure why I detected this, but it was sort of obvious...)
> Topic: changing my Friends and Family numbers.
> Problem: girl on the other end of the phone was just on 'happy juice' and was not really taking my details down properly. Consequently, the confirmation letter (actually two letters sent by mistake) showed a host of wrong numbers entered and she even charged me for a product I did not ask for (F&F is free, of course).
> That really left me thinking:
>
> 1. I like BT even less than before, a lot less.
> 2. They are going down the tubes by outsourcing telesales/customer service to inferior companies.
> 3. The world is generally degenerating.
>
> That last one is surprising because my overall impression of customer service via telephone is that it is so, so much better than 'the old days' when you rang a local branch of a bank, telephone company, gas company, etc and spoke to an untrained person who might be having an off-day and whose job was not to answer phones but to administer things or be a secretary. I am also impressed by the high standards of 'niceness' you get, even at 1 am in the morning from my bank (probably after several hours of listening to irate people). This gives me a lot of faith in 'mass training techniques' for average-skilled individuals. Overall, very positive. But not BT.

Quality content certainly means having well-written, well-designed Web pages. It's a false economy not to use a professional writer to put together your text, or a professional designer to develop the look of the pages. But it is most of all about doing what you say you will do – delivering on the promise.

Communication filters

The relationship with the customer is a two-way affair. It should be a dialogue, not a lecture. Content is also a two-way concept. It's not just a matter of your contribution, but also of the customer's. However, there is a problem here. People filter their communications, unconsciously describing not 'the' world but 'their' world, which is inevitably coloured by their experiences and attitudes. This is done in good faith (usually – there are circumstances when customers actively lie, as discussed in the next section).

This problem has been well analysed because it lies at the heart of knowledge management. We can't contain details of the whole world and everything that ever happens in our brain. There's simply too much information involved. Instead we have mental maps and models that approximate to what the real world is like. A simple example is the process of switching on a PC, for which you could in theory provide detailed information. It would involve the exact area of the surface of the casing within which you need to position your fingertip. It would include the range of forces with which you should press the button so that it is strong enough to register with the switch, but not so strong that the switch is damaged. It would include the instruction to remove your finger from the switch, if appropriate. The detailed information for this incredibly simple task would run to pages of specifications, but the mental model is just 'I press the switch.'

Such models may be necessary to cope with the complexity of the real world, but they also create problems. There are an awful lot of assumptions in the simplistic model. When customers speak to you or send you an e-mail, they are operating on the basis of assumptions. Consultant Nick Duffill lists the characteristics that can apply to customer assumptions:

- The customers' world is *the* world to them.
- The customers are certain it's not their problem.
- The assumptions are made in good faith.
- The customers think something is not relevant.
- The customers think something else *is* relevant and are trying to help.
- The customers are trying to hide their ignorance:
  - from you;
  - from their peers and managers;
  - especially if the consequences are significant;
  - especially if they know they have not tried to help themselves.
- The customers are trying to minimize their responsibilities.
- The customers are trying to maximize the seriousness of the problem.

- The customers hope that you will be more motivated to help.
- The customers represent unfounded expectations as 'obvious essentials'.

Let's take some examples of customers filtering information to make this clearer. Fred doesn't mention that he is using a pre-release version of the product as you may realize he hasn't paid for it. Gill talks about everything that has gone wrong with her car, without mentioning that she has never had it serviced or put any oil in it. Oliver says that his entire business depends on delivery of this package tomorrow morning (it's actually his godson's birthday present). Or take the example in the horror story below.

Horror story

The static charge

This is a call centre experience of customer models:

A few years ago I worked in a call centre. I supported the repairs and mainte-nance module of a housing management system and spent quite a lot of time talking to non-technical people.

On one occasion a team leader for one of our customers called asking for advice on how to prevent a particular member of staff from crashing her PC with static electricity. Apparently the machine had an intermittent fault and they thought it was down to the end user being statically charged. They got her to only wear cotton clothes, to change her shampoo, clothes powder and soap. They made her sit on a plastic mat isolating her from the rest of the department but still the PC kept crashing and so they apologetically turned to us for advice. The problem of course turned out to be hardware related.

In the static charge example, the customers had made incorrect assump-tions about the cause of the PC crash. In this case, they had taken the prob-lem into their own hands, but imagine a similar example where the customers ring up the call centre and describe what they think they are see-ing. If they say, 'We've got problems with really bad static in the office – do you have any suggestions on how to reduce it?', the agent is unlikely to think of PC hardware faults.

Removing the filters

An important part of ensuring quality of content is working through the filters that customers impose in their conversations with agents. This is a matter of getting the bigger picture – pushing out the boundaries beyond the simple description of what is happening. A key to making this work is understanding the why and what of their problem. Don't let them leave you with the symptoms alone. What are they actually trying to achieve? What were they doing when the problem arose? Did anything else happen around that time? How does the problem get in the way of their goal? Try to get a feel for why they are telling you that particular set of information. There will often be a reason, and it will help a lot if you can uncover it. You need to get as much background as you can from those involved.

Note that customers may oppose you on some of these points. Their response to questions about the bigger picture might be, 'None of your business – this is my problem; fix it.' Under such circumstances it is necessary to explain gently that you can't fix the problem without understanding the circumstances leading up to it – that is all you are trying to do, but without that information you will probably fail.

An important issue here is one of problem ownership. Customers may just want to dump the problem on you, but in practice they are still involved in it and may have given you only a subset of the information. The ideal position is to share responsibility for the issue. It isn't your problem or the customer's; it's a joint problem.

An essential to achieving this is establishing that you are both on the same side. As long as there is an 'us and them' mentality, customers won't be able to share the problem with you properly. The outcome, all too often, is the sort of angry response detailed in Chapter 6. Customers have to be aware of their role, which includes letting you know what is happening. If you aren't on the same side, failure is an almost inevitable outcome.

Lying customers

Sometimes you will have to deal with more than a communication problem. Some customers will tell you lies. Don't let this lead you to assume all your customers are liars. The aim should be to trust the customer as much as is practical. When you use security, make sure that it is clearly aimed at protecting the customer, rather than you. Once again you are trying to stay away from the 'us and them' stance. Often it is better to give customers the benefit of the doubt, rather than assume that they are out to fleece you.

Horror story

Taken to the cleaners

A major dry-cleaning chain appears on a TV consumer show to defend itself from customer complaints. 'Customer service is very important to us,' it says. 'We have millions of garments brought in and very few complaints. If customers have a problem they need only get the damage assessed by an independent assessor, and if we're proved to be at fault, we'll compensate them in full.'

If there are only a few complaints, why not assume customers are in the right? Why make them prove (at their own expense) that your company made a mistake? Customer service? I don't think so.

The example of the dry cleaners does not involve an invisible customer, but the lesson is clear. It may be that a small proportion of those 'very few' complaints were from liars, but this approach associated all the genuine customers with them. It's no way to keep customers.

9

Who are those customers?

The second bridging chapter looks at customer knowledge. What can you know about remote customers? How can the information be collected and made appropriately available? We examine the distinction between the information that is collected because it's easy to collect and the information that could be genuinely useful.

Knowing your customer

For a long time now, those involved in customer service have realized the importance of knowing their customers. The better you know your customers, the more you can match your products and services to their needs. The more you can develop a relationship with your customers, the more they are likely to have loyalty – not a common factor any more in a world of faceless me-too retailers, carbon-copy services, and copycat manufacturers. It's hard to put concrete value on 'knowing your customer', but most customer-savvy organizations rate it very highly.

You only have to go into a supermarket to feel the full force of the attempt to know the customer: loyalty cards; clubs for gardeners or people with young children; banks; online services; charge cards. All these have service and sales issues, but the prime driver is getting to know customers better. Online bookstore Amazon is said no longer to regard itself as a bookseller, but as the owner of a list of customers to whom it can sell a whole range of products and services. Building on but keeping its customer list secure is a major part of its commercial strategy.

Invisible customers present immediate difficulties in building a relationship, as we saw in Chapter 6. However, those dealing with remote customers have some advantages too. On a telephone you may well be able to recognize customers from their telephone number. If not, you have at least the ability to ask who they are, which you cannot do with a browser in a store. Online the potential is even greater. You can watch what customers do, building a profile of their interests. You can ask them to fill in quick forms. You can change what they see depending on this experience. The opportunities are there, as we will see later in the chapter.

Managing your knowledge

Knowing someone implies dealing with knowledge, a thorny subject if all the books about knowledge management on the business bookshelves are anything to go by. Whether or not you think knowledge management is just another name for what we've always done, it provides lessons that are of value in managing customer relationships. We have already discussed one in the previous chapter – the way information is always viewed through our personal filters. Other important factors are the difficulties of handling knowledge as an isolated entity, and knowledge representation.

Isolating knowledge is the corporate dream. To take an expert and somehow cream off all the knowledge, structure it and put it into a computer would be a major breakthrough. Experts are expensive, in short supply, and subject to human frailties. If their expertise could be isolated, we would not need to rely on risky human resources.

It was this vision that drove the major attempts to develop artificial intelligence systems in business in the 80s and early 90s. Yet today in the business environment, experts are more valued than ever. We have a knowledge-based economy, where expertise is at a premium. What happened was complex. There was an element of self-defence about the way experts co-operated with knowledge-gathering ('elicitation') sessions. Few experts were likely to give all their personal secrets to a machine. As it happened, very few of them could anyway.

The process of garnering knowledge and putting it into a computer is usually one of collecting rules and instances that will illustrate what to do in a certain circumstance. Few experts proved able to do this. It isn't just that being an expert at doing something doesn't of itself make that person a great communicator, but also that most expertise operates partially at a subconscious level. People react in a certain way, influenced by teaching and experience, but don't know what triggers that response.

Worse problems hit the knowledge engineers. Even when they managed to extract knowledge so effectively that the computer could equal a human expert's decisions, the quality of the computer's expertise seemed to deteriorate over time. The problem is that knowledge has a live component. It is constantly monitoring what happens, pulling in extra up-to-date information and modifying itself. As soon as the computers codified the knowledge, it was frozen. The expert, on the other hand, continues to modify his or her behaviour as a result of experience.

The result of this painful learning curve is to understand that a good knowledge system can either be based solely on a human being, or be a hybrid system involving a human and a computer, but it can't be provided by a computer alone. Translating this into a call centre or Web support environment, a knowledge base is a great support tool for your expert engineers, but it can't replace them. It can help less expert people deal with problems (or help customers directly), but only if it is constantly being used and updated by the 'real' experts. Similarly a customer relationship management system is only going to be as good as the people experts who use and modify the information.

Ease and value

There is a trade-off in every information system, but particularly so when the information is about customers. It is between ease of obtaining the information, and the value it has for the company. It is often tempting to build systems around what is easy to obtain, rather than the information that will actually make a difference. Take the information you display about customers when they ring you up, which we'll consider further in the next section. What's easy to show? Customers' telephone numbers. What do you actually want to know? Customers' names, what they mean to your company, any history they may have and why they are calling you today. Much of that second list is achievable but, all too often, lazily developed systems will not stretch far beyond the 'give them a number' phase.

When looking at dealing with customers on the phone or online, the starting point should be 'What information would be valuable to us?' Resist the urge to be an information squirrel – always a danger in the knowledge management arena. If you are selling financial services, you aren't interested in inside-leg measurements. Don't try to list every possible piece of information you might be able to glean. Instead concentrate on the facts and feelings (don't forget feelings just because we are dealing with information; feelings come into buying decisions in a big way) that are likely to influence customers' interactions with your company.

The specific cut of information required will often differ depending on the nature of the customer contact. If you are providing customer support for a piece of computer software, you want to know as much as possible about the computer that is being used, what the customer does with it and any previous problems he or she has contacted you about. If, on the other hand, you are selling stationery, you are much more interested in the sort of products the customer has bought before and the type of business involved. If you are putting in a new computer system to deal with customer information, a prime requirement is the ability of different parts of the organization to take very different cuts on the data.

Pop till you drop

Popping is a prime activity in any well-run inbound call centre. A call comes in. If the system can recognize the number, it should pop the customer's information on the screen. This should be a matter of course – it is amazing that many telephone companies, for instance, still ask customers which number they are dialling on. It isn't a cast-iron method of identification. If you are dealing with business-to-business commerce, then it might be enough to know the company whose phone is being used, but for personal customers you can't be sure the person you have information about is the one using the phone. Some checks will normally be necessary, but an automatic pop means that you've got the basic information in front of you immediately.

If the number can't be recognized, some form of identifier needs to be used, but once that has been provided, the information should all be popped on the screen as soon as possible. If the call needs to be passed on, that same screen pop should pass with the call to whoever takes over. As soon as customers have to repeat their details to a second person, the system has failed.

A final consideration on the popping process is the form of identifier used. Because they're easy to handle on keypads, we tend to use numbers for identification – often long, unmanageable numbers (one US state had driver's licence numbers that would have been suitable if every atom in our galaxy had required a licence). Even a credit card number is much too big to cope with easily – credit card numbers are entered into a keypad incorrectly about one in six times. This shouldn't be surprising. We use words and pictures to convey ideas, not numbers.

If customer service really matters to you, consider moving to a text-oriented form of identifier. Let customers choose their own. People usually remember their e-mail address more easily than their telephone number (and their telephone number more easily than their client code with the insurance company) – partly because it's text and partly because they have usually chosen part of it themselves. There's no reason why your company's client references have to be automatically generated. If you have to use numbers, why not choose a number customers already know – their telephone number? If you need several people on the same number, stick an initial on the end.

Getting personal

So you've collected lots of great information about your customers. When they call you, the screen pops it up. How do you use it? Do you say, 'Hello, Mrs Smith, glad you've called us again for the 15th time this month. I see you take sugar in your coffee – that's great to know'? Maybe not. There's a big-brother feeling of 'we know all about you', the sugar in the coffee bit is irrelevant, and telling her she has called 15 times this month sounds like a criticism. The information is there to help agents make the call more effective for customers, and to make a more personal touch possible.

The lightest approach is simply to allow the agent to get in the right frame of mind. When using caller ID on a domestic phone, in most cases you don't pick it up and say, 'Hello, Fred.' Instead you use the knowledge that it's going to be Fred on the other end of the line to be prepared for one of his long monologues (or occasionally to pretend you're out).

The next level might be to make use of relevant facts, but only as and when required. You don't need to tell customers that you know their make of car unless they ask you if you've got any tyres. Then it's reasonable to say, 'Is that for your 1998 Galaxy?' or whatever.

A further level is a more proactive approach. 'While you're on, I've noticed that you've had some problems with your fax machine lately. How's it going now? Have you considered moving over to plain paper fax? They're much easier to keep running.' This shouldn't always be a sales push. Sometimes it could be a genuine enquiry without any follow-up sales comment. It might be asking about the customer, or about your products and services. 'How are you finding our legal advice line? Any suggestions for improvements?'

The final level is the truly personal touch. I go to a barber in a nearby village to get my hair cut. When I go in, the barber might say, 'How are the children doing now they're at school?' or 'Are you still working from home?' She knows me well enough to ask sensible personalized questions, and it very much reinforces the business relationship. The same can be done in the telephone context, with one proviso: personal information should only be discussed by the same individuals who got the information from customers in the first place. Even if they do not remember the customers, the system should be able to identify who recorded the data.

Imagine that amongst the background information on a customer, the agent sees she has just moved house. 'How's the new house going?' the agent might ask. The customer is immediately wary. How does this person know these personal details? And the more personal the detail (say about spouse or children), the greater the suspicion. If, however, the agent can say, 'Weren't you in the process of moving house last time I spoke to you?' things are much easier. The agent becomes a real person on the end of the line, one the customer has spoken to before. Unless the information is very memorable, it is probably best to put it across in a slightly hesitant way like this. Even though the customer may be aware of customer databases, the pretence is being kept up that the agent has remembered this fact about the customer through normal human interest. With lots of customers there might be some confusion, so 'Weren't you moving?' is more acceptable than 'You moved house on the 16th September, didn't you?' – that sort of precision seems unnatural.

Quick tips

Small-company feel

Personalization is about getting the small-company feel – the comfort of dealing with an actual person who knows you. Peter Cox, CEO of literary agency Litopia, has some interesting observations.

> The Internet exposes you and the weakest aspect of your company as never before. I think you have to view it, essentially, as a one-to-one communications medium, and I also think a lot of problems stem from the inability of large corporate behemoths to understand this. Small companies deal with everyone on a personal basis. Large companies only relate to percentages, market share, market research, and majorities. As CEO of a smallish company, I will spend an inordinate amount of time on individuals, even when I can see no direct reward for doing so. In a large company, I'd probably be sacked.

Managing the mail

To manage a customer relationship well involves recognizing as many as possible of your communications with the same customer and linking them together. Having a history of interaction can be intensely valuable in making the customer service go right. Yet some companies go out of their way to make this difficult. I regularly deal with a large PR company. Each of its 30 or 40 consultants has his or her own contact database. Every time you deal with someone new, they ask for your address and telephone number. They have no idea of what the agency has done for you before. At best it is an irritation for the customer, at worst a nightmare.

E-mail has the big advantage over many other means of communication of being relatively easy to manage automatically in the context of customer information. From the incoming mail address you may well be able to identify the customer, and so be able to tie the e-mail into the customer's history. There is a slight snag here, particularly with non-corporate customers. E-mail addresses have a habit of changing frequently, especially while 'free' ISPs and e-mail services like Hotmail provide instant extra addresses. This means it is essential that a system managing mail can cope with a range of addresses for the same person, but many addresses will be recognized, providing instant tie-back to customer data.

It's no longer acceptable to have a customer database that can't integrate e-mails, calls and every other means of contact with the customer. Sometimes this is managed by having a secondary system piggyback on the 'legacy' (out-of-date but difficult-to-replace) customer database. However it is achieved, it is an essential.

Cookies and customization

Personalization of a Web site is important, as its aim is to achieve what Bill Wittenberg of Art Technology Group, a company specializing in customer relationship management on the Web, has called 'customer stickiness'. The problem with the Web from the vendor's viewpoint is that it's so easy to click away elsewhere, out of your grasp, perhaps for ever. If there is a way to make your Web site sticky without irritating the customers, it will be well worth it.

That 'without irritating the customers' bit is worth repeating. There is a very easy way to stick to customers: whenever they click on a link from your site, you actually keep them at your site and display the new site in a part of the screen (a frame). This doesn't stop people typing a new address or using a bookmark, but it can hold on to people using your site's resources. The trouble is, it also clogs up a fair amount of the screen. If the second site you link to does it as well (and so on), before long there's no screen left. Stickiness through frames is a good example of how not to do it.

The way Wittenberg recommends you hold on to customers is always to be giving them value back, to make it worth their while to undertake an action. For instance, if they are filling in a form, they should get something in return for it of direct benefit. Personalization can add that value through a key factor – speed. There's probably nothing you can do with personalization that customers can't do themselves in time, but you can save them the time and reduce the chance of them clicking elsewhere.

Amazon has a very specific aspect of personalization in 1-Click; but getting customers to what they want smoothly and quickly isn't just about the purchasing part of the experience. For instance, imagine you wanted to find out about a laptop and visited two sites – Dell, a firm specializing in personal computers, and IBM, a company with a vast product range amongst which laptops are but a very small part. The challenge IBM faces is to make it as easy for customers to get to the laptop information as when dealing with a much more focused site like Dell's.

There is a limit to how much personalization you can do on a first visit – though an integrated customer relationship management system may be able to recognize a customer's e-mail address and pull information from other sources – but on subsequent visits, if you have managed to get a clear picture of who someone is, you can give them immediate access to the parts of the site that are most likely to interest them. It is possible to overdo this, of course. If customers go to the laptop part of the IBM site on their first visit, and then next time they visit all they can see is laptops, it will be very irritating if this time they are looking to buy a mainframe. On the other hand, it will be very effective if there is a clear button for the laptop section on the front page that wasn't there before.

At the heart of personalization is the cookie, a small file on the user's PC that the browser is authorized to write to. Generally customers' PCs are well protected against intrusion from the Internet, but most people accept cookies (browsers can be set to refuse them, though – you can't force them on people, just sell their advantages). A cookie is often used to identify the particular position of a customer in your site, but the best use you can make of it is if you tie a key in the cookie to your customer relationship database, so you can go far beyond this and tailor pages according to the information you hold (and continue to collect) about the customer.

As with any invisible customer, you can't be absolutely sure that the person you think you are dealing with is the one who was last using that computer. A reasonable compromise is that adopted by many sites of saying something like 'Welcome back, Brian. If you aren't Brian Clegg, please click here.'

Hot news, just in

Although tailoring a Web site is at the leading edge of practical customization, it doesn't pay to miss out on the cheap and cheerful complementary options available. Specifically, e-mail alerts should be an effective part of your managed relationship. While junk mail is generally shunned, regular updates on a subject of interest are very popular. It means that customers don't have to go out hunting on the Web, but that the update can be brought to them. With HTML e-mail (see Chapter 7), you can even make those updates Web pages in their own right.

E-mail updating has to be managed carefully. The dividing line between updates and spam (unwanted mass mailing) is thin. The principal rules for keeping on the right side of the line are to ensure that customers actively ask for the update (you can push its benefits as much as you like on your site, but don't start it automatically as a result of gleaning an e-mail address), and to tailor content as much as possible. The more the update can match customers' requirements – especially if it can be done without them spending 20 minutes filling in an online questionnaire – the better chance it will be appreciated and kept up. Keeping on the list has to be under customers' control. Resist the temptation to make it difficult to unsubscribe – this just irritates.

Painless extraction

The more information you can get about customers, the better picture you can build and the more effectively you can tailor your invisible customer service to their requirements. Some of this information can be picked up in the background. What pages do they browse? How long do they spend where? But Web browsers only give a very limited set of information. Other information might be taken from conventional customer databases if you can match the online customer to the offline, but you will generally have to resort to a form.

The tips in Chapter 5 for designing an e-mail form apply equally well here, particularly the need to keep it short. The less you ask, the more likely you are to get the form filled in. Probably the most important thing to ask for is the name and e-mail address – given that and cookies, you have the vehicle for easy communication and effective personalization.

Making use of the knowledge

This laboriously built knowledge about customers is not assembled out of mere curiosity or a big-brother-like urge to infringe personal freedom and privacy. The whole point is to be able to provide customers with the best experience – to make customer service superb throughout the relationship.

Having a relationship implies having more than a one-off contact. Bearing in mind the importance of the customer's lifetime value, it's not surprising how important building a relationship is. A popular model of the invisible customer relationship is shown in the diagram below.

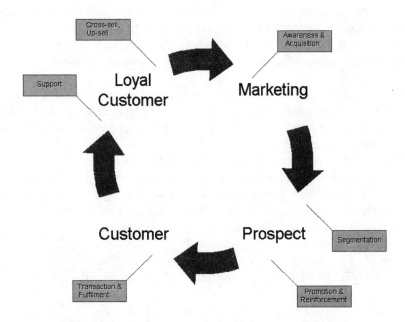

Figure 9.1 Remote customer relationship model (courtesy Art Technology Group)

Taking a truly customer-driven approach will allow the relationship to change at each stage of the process, tailoring the Web site or the phone conversation to meet the specific requirements of customers or potential customers. At each stage of the relationship cycle, customers will be looking for different things from your company. In the model above the main events are:

- *Awareness and acquisition:* These events apply typically to the first few visits to a site. Visitors may be browsing by chance or looking for specific content or a product that interests them. If they find something of interest, they may return and perhaps become regular visitors.
- *Segmentation:* At this point the company knows a little more about potential customers. Visitors may have provided some information about themselves via a registration form or by making a purchase. Using this information, the business manager can make decisions about the meaning of visitor behaviour and create business rules based on that behaviour.
- *Promotion and reinforcement:* It is at this stage that visitors and the business really interact. Visitors have provided some information about their interests, and the business manager has set up some rules about what type of content or product information to show visitors with certain patterns. This is the point where dynamic content or promotion information can help move site visitors towards purchase or repeat purchase.
- *Transaction and fulfilment:* Customers have decided to make a commitment to the business, maybe through a purchase or site membership. That purchase needs to be fulfilled, based on the visitor's profile and transaction information.
- *Support:* One factor in building long-standing customer relationships is the ability to support customers after the transaction. It is important to track, store and analyse information about customers in order to provide the service that will keep them coming back to the site.
- *Cross-sell and up-sell:* At this point in the customer lifecycle, the business is building on existing relationships. With knowledge of site visitors' past purchase history and expressed needs, the business manager can deliver the most appropriate information to keep them loyal.

ATG, which promotes this model and provides Web software to support it, emphasizes that it's important to note that a customer relationship that isn't managed well could fail at any of these stages. It's only by keeping on top of the whole cycle that it is possible to reap the benefits of customer relationship management – retention and realization of lifetime value.

Measure, measure, measure

There are times when it's easy to think that all customer service people are interested in is measurement. It's certainly true that in many call centres and Web service sites, metrics are given more importance than customers themselves. We will examine taking a balanced scorecard approach to measurement in Chapter 16. For the moment, it is worth noting that a good Web site provides much tighter metrics than practically any other method of monitoring customers. It is much easier, for instance, with an Internet mailing to check the percentage of people responding than it is with a conventional postal mailshot. The Internet can provide instant feedback on what is happening.

Say your company wanted to run a promotion. It is possible to test out the promotion for an hour or a day on the Web and get instant analysis of results before putting money into a full-scale exercise. Perhaps it was too costly for the returns, or perhaps no one was interested. There has never been such an immediate way of testing the impact of a promotion or new line. While the benefits of some metrics related to call centre throughput are dubious, there's no doubting the huge impact that Web-based measurement of response can bring.

As always with statistics based on a limited sample, it is worth remembering that Web users are not 'typical'. They are more likely to hold professional positions and be well educated than the population at large. This may not be a disadvantage for most campaigns, but it is worth bearing in mind. Web-derived statistics are fine if they are to provide deductions about Web-based business, but they are not representative of the entire customer base.

10

You can't get the staff

Staff present a problem for those involved with providing service to the invisible customer. Being an agent is seen as a dead-end job, or just a temporary post before a real career can be set up. This chapter looks at the dangers inherent in this view, and at doing something about it.

Growth business

In a report by the UK Call Centre Association, it was estimated that more than 2 per cent of the UK workforce are involved in call centre work. To get the most out of this grouping is challenging. Call centre work is not seen as a long-term career. In fact, the work has been demonized as dead-end, where all you can look forward to is abuse from the customers. The working environment is portrayed as a sweatshop that forces calls on the agents with production-line monotony. If there's one concept that sums up the image of call centres, it is timed toilet breaks.

There is some evidence, as we will see later in the chapter, that much of this picture is a myth, but it is a well-established myth. It seems unlikely that many young people, when considering careers, would list 'working in a call centre' high on their list. Overcoming the image will take time and effort, but is necessary. Great call centre staff make more than a little difference: they can transform the effectiveness and customer satisfaction produced by a call centre. Note, by the way, that while most of this chapter is specific to the call centre and hence voice handling, it is increasingly common to combine Internet support and the call centre, and the chapter is equally applicable to both.

Any image change will not be achieved by advertising or glossy brochures. In the beginning, it has to come from within. A workforce of this size has a large word-of-mouth impact on the world, and increasing the motivation of the workforce has to be the starting point for changing the image of the job. Increased motivation has other benefits too. Not only does it make the job sound better, it results in more effective service for customers, and hence improves their satisfaction. This feeds back to the staff themselves, both in the responses they get from customers and in any incentive schemes that are operated, resulting in better retention of staff and even, to close the loop, better motivation.

Much of the next three chapters will be concerned with factors that increase motivation, but we will start by looking at some of the negatives and what can be done about them.

They don't stay

Call-centre work is usually thought to involve high turnover rates. This was borne out in a survey taken by the Call Centre Association in 1998. The results are shown in figure 10.1.

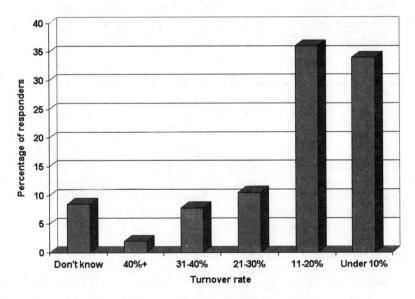

Figure 10.1 Annual call-centre staff turnover

That any companies recorded turnovers in excess of 40 per cent each year is quite staggering. In most other jobs, turnover rates at these levels would be considered dangerously high. Operating at such levels implies that the job is one that is incapable of retaining the interest of those involved, is abysmally managed or burns out the individuals in a short time. There is a fourth possibility, that the job is a clear stepping stone to a more advanced role, which most staff move through very quickly, but that is unlikely in this instance.

The impact of such high turnover rates on the quality of service from the call centre will probably be significant. Consider those operating at over 40 per cent. This implies that perhaps half the staff have been in the job for less than a year. Allowing for training time, the chances of getting through to an agent with negligible experience are high. This is likely to mean limited knowledge of the company, its products and its services, and may well also mean a more rigid and ineffective approach to dealing with customers.

A dead-end job

Because the quality of agents can make a huge difference to customer service, there is a need to make sure that being an agent isn't seen as a dead-end job. This can't be done with labels alone, though some care should be taken about how your agents are referred to in company literature. Instead, preventing the dead-end job requires real action.

Quick tips

No more dead-end job

- *Clear training prospects:* Training is covered in detail in the next chapter, but it should be an identified part of the job and should be ongoing, both in details of products and services, and in customer service skills. This training opportunity should be known about by all agents.
- *Empowerment to match responsibility:* This is covered in Chapter 12. The agent should have the flexibility to be able to act in the most appropriate way for the company and customers. The job is not about being a human answering machine, but an active face of the company.

- *Opportunity for variety:* Agents should have a chance to move around different roles within the site. They should be more like a modern car-assembly worker, taking on different tasks in the process, rather than a 20th-century assembly-line worker. At least once a week, there should be the chance to do something different.
- *Clear routes into different parts of the company:* A good agent should have prospects in many other parts of the company, as agents know customers better than most. If a fair percentage of the call centre's turnover isn't going into the company, a powerful resource is being wasted.
- *Recruitment on a broad range of skills.*
- *Provision of opportunities to learn new technologies:* See the expansion of the call centre into Web work as an opportunity to develop your agents.

Whom do we employ?

The Call Centre Association's 1998 survey gives a reasonable picture of the age distribution in UK call centres. This was based on a split of around 65 per cent of staff being female.

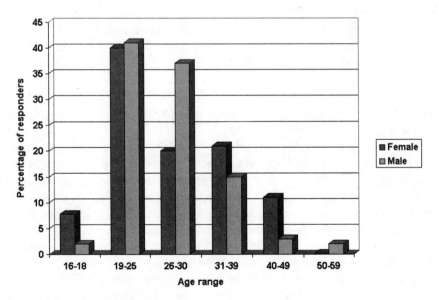

Figure 10.2   Staff age groups

While agents are largely not teenagers, the bulk of agents fit into a young adult bracket. This is interesting when looking at the experience of the impact of age on quality of customer service. A number of large retailers have experimented with using older staff, particularly in the sort of roles where customers are likely to ask for advice. Older staff have proved more patient, give a more positive and informal service and are considered more appropriate to go to for advice. It is interesting in such circumstances how few call centre staff are over 40, with hardly any women over 50.

An envisaged problem here might be that call centre jobs are often in hi-tech areas, or involve the use of technology. Older people are seen as being uncertain with technology, and can be slower to feel comfortable with computers. However, this limitation is not reflected in any lesser ability to handle the technology required for call centre work, with appropriate training.

That actively seeking out older agents is worth while is emphasized by David Firth, now a consultant but for a number of years a call centre manager. 'We found it well worth targeting middle-aged agents. Most of our staff were young jobbing actors, but when we got middle-aged staff the returns were much better.'

What makes a good agent?

A good agent is a 'people person' first and foremost. Agents need to be able to cope with customers at their worst. A good role model in this respect is the top rate airline flight attendant, who can cope with immense pressures and still enjoy dealing with people. Those who are really good with people will not be happy with spouting a script, but will make sure that what they have to say fits naturally with their own speech patterns, and will vary what they say to fit requirements.

In most agent jobs, though, interpersonal skills are not enough; there's nothing worse than talking to an agent, however much sympathy and empathy they exude, who has less idea about the technical question you are asking than you do yourself. Throw into the mix a low-stress personality, excellent time management, creativity, flexibility and an urge to finish, and you've got the makings of a great agent.

As with most jobs involving skill, there are a few call centre staff who stand out from the crowd. What is rarely recognized by companies or incentive schemes is just how outstanding the key players are. In a job like software programming, a star can be five times as productive as an ordinary competent programmer. Similarly, a call centre star will not just improve on the average by a few per cent but by 10s or even 100s, whether the measure is getting business on cold calls or customer satisfaction when giving service.

Ex-call centre manager David Firth is clear about this. 'It isn't about the fact that you generally get bad people, but that one or two are stars. They are real communicators – other people can't do it the same way. Whatever they do, they sound like they are reading a script, but the stars make you feel that you are having a real conversation.'

Taking it further

If you are to get and keep the right people for the job, perhaps it is time to re-think the whole way agents are recruited and rewarded. Traditionally (outbound) call centre agents were often jobbing actors, because they were always in need of work and were good at reading scripts. That's fine for the old breed of agent, but did not produce true company ambassadors. Recruitment should be aiming instead at the sort of people who really get a buzz out of giving good customer service.

Similarly, the reward structure needs to be reconsidered. Those stars that David Firth mentioned should be rewarded well enough to ensure that being an agent for (say) 10 years doesn't seem an unreasonable plan. That means great pay, but also better non-monetary rewards and a bonus scheme that really reflects the agent's value to the company.

Most of all we need to see the job made more attractive to attract a better class of agent: better working conditions, more flexibility, more opportunity to perform different roles within the site. Expensive? Maybe, but it's the only way out of the vicious spiral.

11

Training and learning

Training and learning combined are vital in providing good service to the remote customer. This applies to the staff themselves, their management and supporters – and possibly even the customers. One aspect of training should be how to find out about, and keep up to date with, the competition, both to be able to show knowledgeably how your products stand out... and to be able to recommend the opposition if necessary.

People off the street

It sometimes seems as if the policy of call centres is to take the cheapest people they can off the street, show them how to answer a telephone or run through a list of outbound calls, give them a script and leave them to it. This year alone, I have had dealings with call centres where agents have:

- put down the phone without a word as soon as it was clear I wasn't a potential sale;
- been rude;
- told me I had done the wrong thing;
- ignored my reply to a question and ploughed on with an inflexible and irrelevant script;
- lied to me.

Any training they had had was not showing. If your agents are to be effective ambassadors for the company, they need layers of training that are likely to go on through their entire time with the site.

Basic training

The core training for agents should reflect the nature of the job. Agents are there to provide an effective service to customers in as cost-effective a way as is possible. To provide any service to human beings requires communications skills. These are particularly important in a relationship that is channelled through a narrow vehicle like the telephone or the Web. Alongside the basics of how to communicate effectively sits an understanding of people. Agents have to deal with people who are angry or frustrated – some basic psychology and people skills are very valuable.

The specifics of communication are likely to need verbal skills and, in many cases, writing skills too. Yet alone, communication isn't worth a lot. Without content, communication becomes small talk – fine for a chat line, but not the business of customer service. The agent needs sufficient knowledge about the company's products and services to be able to fulfil his or her role. The specifics of sales or support may define exactly what level of knowledge is required, but it's certain that there will be some requirement. Less obvious, but still essential as we will examine later, is the need for knowledge about competitors' products.

Although there are many other skills that might be valuable, probably the next most important is time management. Agents need to make most appropriate use of their time to keep their customers happy. Good time management will help avoid the frustration of customers having their request for help ignored by your company.

Understanding your products and services

Of all the necessary training, the most obvious is a knowledge of your products and services. There should be no doubt at all that it is impossible to sell a product without a good understanding of the product. Even more so, any attempt to support a product without a good understanding (both technical and practical) is futile. Nevertheless, episodes like the horror story below are all too common.

Horror story

By the book

The offending company was not identified here, but the mistakes they made were common and easily countered.

> When I was systems programming at Ferranti we would ring in on the software support contract. Within about four hours (they were quite good at hitting the deadlines) you'd get a call back from the 'support professional'. It usually appeared to be someone who'd just done the course for the subject in hand, and who'd read the manual back to you.
>
> After about 10 minutes of 'Yes, I've read that and tried it – it doesn't work' he'd decide he couldn't cope and pass you on to a more senior expert who could occasionally help. (I say 'he' – they all seemed to be male.) After a while we learned to hoard names of people who could really help, and ask for them by name.

Note: timing is important, but not sufficient without content. It is rarely enough to use the same manual as the customer, and can seem particularly offensive if the customer has already done this. Regular customers can often benefit from having names or direct numbers for appropriate contacts.

That staff should be expected to support a product without anything more to help them than the basic instruction book is the cheap and disastrous approach to support. It certainly doesn't cost a lot in training, but it has almost no value to customers except for very basic support. Training in products and services operates at a number of levels. Exactly what is needed depends on the role the agent is expected to fulfil, but virtually all agents will benefit by having more product knowledge. The spectrum of training runs something like this:

1. *Basic background:* The sort of information to be gathered from a company's handouts and catalogues.
2. *Background explained:* The same basic information as in 1, but with an understanding of the meanings and implications of the information. With level 1, you would know that your company made left-handed thrupple nuts. With level 2, you would know that a thrupple nut is a special reverse-screw lock nut used to keep the tops on weather vanes.

3. *Detailed product knowledge:* This is particularly important for sales. It means not just understanding the products at brochure level, but able to discuss the pros and cons of the different features.
4. *Application knowledge:* Not just knowing the product in isolation, but also something about how the product is used in practice and the implications. It helps if the agent has actually tried out the product or service.
5. *Competitor knowledge:* Throw in knowledge of the competitors' products so that sensible comparisons can be made.
6. *Basic support:* As well as all the above, having a knowledge of the most common problems customers have with the products and services, and clear ideas of how to fix them.
7. *Intermediate support:* Adds to the basic a more general technical knowledge of the product and its application, so that unexpected problems can be diagnosed and corrected.
8. *High-level support:* Adds to the intermediate an intimate knowledge of the technical workings of the product. The agent is able if necessary to make (or to talk the customer through) modifications to the product to fix problems.

While this list is not exclusive, it provides a good picture of the sorts of training that are likely to be necessary in the company's products and services. Note that being a service business doesn't exclude your agents from needing this knowledge. It is simpler to describe the training in terms of physical products, but all the levels of requirement will be the same, from insurance cover to an industrial cleaning contract.

Understanding people

We will deal with the requirement to train in communications skills separately, but there is an underlying need to be able to understand people, for example in the following situations: dealing with angry or confused customers; defusing a hostile situation; and getting an understanding of the buying relationship, making sure that customers see what they want to see. It's the least specific of the training topics, so there won't be much said about it, but it is at the centre of the agent's training requirement.

Time management

Time management has been popular as a management skill for a long time, although it tends to be presented as a boring subject. If you see time management as being purely about juggling appointments, calendars and work plans, it is boring, but seen as an attempt to match what you do to your personal aspirations makes it seem quite different.

From the agent's viewpoint, the need for time management is slightly different from a typical manager's approach. The manager has a set of objectives he or she is trying to achieve, and time management is all about organizing time to maximize the chance of meeting the most important objectives. Agents also have some longer-term objectives, probably related to self-development, that can be ticked off as completed, but much of the requirement is to juggle a lot of small tasks at once and ensure that nothing falls between the cracks. The multitude of small tasks requires a more formal structure, which should be supported by the company's systems. Time management operates here at two levels: agents ensuring that they are succeeding in meeting their goals, and a wider management of floating tasks that may move from agent to agent. Awareness of these two requirements is important in any time management training.

The details of time management are covered in great detail elsewhere (see Appendix 1 for more information), but it shouldn't be considered a second-class skill just because it has an administrative flavour. Time management is not optional for a good agent.

Action station

Agent's goals

If you are an agent, spend a couple of minutes noting down what you think are the main things you are trying to achieve in your job. Combine what you'd like to achieve personally and what you feel the company wants. Keep the list somewhere you can see it when you work. After a few days look for gaps between reality and your list. What's getting in the way?

If you are a manager, jot down a similar set of goals that you think would apply to your agents. Now meet with a number of agents and match your picture against their reality. Again, look for gaps. See which needs fixing – their performance or your ideas.

Speaking skills

For call centre agents, speech is at the centre of the job. As we have noted, in the early days of call centres jobbing actors were often used because of their fluency of speech. With the explosion of call centres, though, there are fewer opportunities to make use of trained speakers. Giving some training, and even filtering out people with inappropriate skills, should be part of the package. Key speech elements are accent, tone, clarity and command of vocabulary.

Accent is a mixed blessing in the call centre. Some accents have been shown to be particularly attractive to callers. In the UK, accents like Highland Scottish, Newcastle, Republic of Ireland and French are all received well. Others, particularly Northern Ireland, Birmingham, Received Pronunciation, Lowland Scottish and Estuarial do not go down so well. While some fine tuning is worth while, what's more essential is to make sure that the accent isn't so strong that it becomes difficult for an ear that isn't in tune with it to understand what is said.

Tone is a more subtle concept, but no less important. The way that the agent speaks can say 'I'm really pleased to be speaking to you' or 'You are a waste of my time. Get on with it.' In part, this message is conveyed by non-verbal communication, whether it's an encouraging noise or a sigh of boredom. More often it is the tone and pace of the speech. It is worth making use of video cameras during training to see the impact of using different tones, and then moving to taped phone exercises to enable agents to have better control of their own tone and to keep it bright and engaging.

Keeping a constant volume is valuable – many people, especially those lacking self-confidence, trail off in volume at the end of a sentence. There is also the presence (or absence) of the hesitation words that litter some speech, for example 'erm' or words that don't add meaning such as 'like' and 'you know'. Use of these punctuation noises can be decreased through training. There is another clarity issue in how special information like numbers and letters is put across. Agents, like airline pilots, may benefit from using the well-known pronunciation alphabet (Alpha, Bravo, Charlie, etc) and stressing the end of the number to help distinguish telephone sound-alikes like 'five' and 'nine'.

Command of vocabulary is more complex than the other skills. It's the ability to use the right word at the right time, so agents don't sound stilted but give the appearance of knowing what they are talking about. It's the ability to pull out an appropriate adjective to describe what is wanted, or to put together a request for information that gets the right answer without offending. Sometimes it can simply be having the right words to make pleasant conversation, rather than sounding like a machine. This is hard to train for, but easier to select for. Often older applicants with a wider experience do better in this area.

Writing skills

Writing ability has not been seen as high on the list of necessary skills for agents, unlike verbal skills and an understanding of the product. This is particularly true in technical fields, where the ability to write comprehensibly has never been highly valued. However, the increasing use of Web sites and particularly e-mail in remote customer service adds a new urgency to the need to be able to write effectively. As we have already seen, a badly composed e-mail can carry unwanted messages, and be uninformative and irritating.

The ideal, of course, is that your agents should all be excellent writers as well as product experts and conversational stars. For a few this will be true, but others will need help. You could have a supervisory editor check all outgoing mail, but this is time-consuming and gives a poor message to your agents about the level of trust you have in them. A better approach is to have appropriate tools, simple training and regular reviews of actual e-mails to recommend improvements.

Quick tips

Better e-mail writing

- Use an e-mail package with as-you-type spell checking and auto-correction for common mistakes.
- Consider spelling errors in e-mails to be as important as errors in a brochure.
- Read each e-mail before sending it. Does it make sense?
- Always attach any mail you are replying to, keeping a trail of conversation.
- Keep the text as simple as possible, avoiding jargon and acronyms.
- Keep sentences short.
- Remember that you are having a dialogue with a human being – don't make it too impersonal.

- Never put anything tongue in cheek or intended to be understood as sarcasm – make it plain, and try to keep a single, clear meaning of what you type.
- If you are asking for information, be as specific as you can. Ask for a PC's 'manufacturer and model number' rather than 'What sort of PC have you?' Being told 'a beige one' helps no one.
- Separate individual parts of the response into paragraphs, divided by a blank line.

Consider this e-mail text. It was the response to a query sent to the e-mail support section of the Web page of a major online insurance company, complaining about the ineffectiveness of its call-back service.

As received

Thank you for your comments and we appreciate that the way in which you were dealt with was not per your requirements, the Internet team transfer people over to the queue on the toll-free number however if that number is experiencing high national demand the best advice to offer customers is to call the numbers themselves at a quieter time. If the adviser sugggested you call the number yourself, it may be that she was aware of the queues on the telephone.

We apologize for any inconvenience caused. Should you require further assistance with your prospective quotation please call [number] and our advisers will be happy to help.

Many thanks
BigCo Internet Team

How it might have been

Thank you for your comments. I'm sorry we didn't meet your expectations.

Normally, the Internet team transfer people across to the toll-free number, but when there are long queues they recommend callers to ring back

> later. The adviser gave you incorrect information, for which I apologize, but she was trying to save you time.
>
> Thanks for calling, and I hope you will accept our unreserved apologies and try us again in the future – call [number] and our advisers will be happy to help.
>
> Many thanks,
> Sarah-Jane Smith
> BigCo Internet Team

The first sentence of the original is much too long, and combines two totally separate concepts. The bit up to the first comma sympathizes with my treatment, while the bit after the first comma tells me what the Internet team do. These parts are so different it would have been more effective to have put them into a separate paragraph. The whole e-mail would have been better coming from a real person rather than from a team. In my version I have strengthened the rather weak 'we appreciate' to an out-and-out apology. The phrase 'not per your requirements' is clumsy – no one speaks like that. Even the 'meet your expectations' I have substituted verges on the language of business rather than that of normal human beings. Use everyday language as much as possible.

Splitting off the rest of the sentence should be an absolute necessity. It is too long, and it doesn't make sense. The writer should have read back the text before sending it. It gives confusing, unnecessary information. What does 'high national demand' mean, and what do I care about it? How do I know when a 'quieter time' is? It would have been better to have said 'later', as I did, or give specific times. In the final sentence of the main paragraph there's a spelling mistake ('sugggested'), which might have been spotted in a re-read, but would certainly have been picked up if the system had used spell checking.

The other problem with the final sentence is that it undoes any good the apology might have done. I hadn't been told that the queues were busy, but that the agent *couldn't* put me through. This sentence either suggests that I am lying, or simply overlooks the facts and describes what should have happened. Neither is acceptable. In my version the agent accepts that the adviser made a mistake, and apologizes explicitly for it.

I don't think the three apologies in my version of the e-mail are over the top, as this is essentially an e-mail of apology. The central apology is for a specific error, the action of the adviser, and so stands separate from the two framing apologies. The main reason that the apologies work is that they're personal.

It is important to put the message across well and clearly. Good punctuation and grammar are important too when putting across the image of the company. Agents who write to customers should be aware of the basics, so that they don't come up with the sort of mistakes that irritate many readers. They should avoid the 'greengrocer syndrome' – the total misunderstanding of apostrophes in evidence on the boards outside shops ('Carrot's £1 a kilo'); they should know whether to use 'its' or 'it's'; and they should be aware that apostrophes do have a function.

Communication at the centre of learning

It is worth stressing just how important a part communication is in the learning required by those who are to provide service to the invisible customer. In the Call Centre Association survey, it was noted that a lot of the requests from agents for change were about improved communication. The report noted: 'Improved communication can be achieved by providing more opportunities for dialogue and organizational learning.' Communication is involved both in terms of enhancing the communication between agent and customer, and in improved communication between the company and the agent and between agents. This needs support both from systems and from training.

Learning about the competition

All too often agents are ignorant of the other companies and products in their field. Training needs to extend beyond your own company's products and services to take in the competition – and not just their good points (see the comments on silver bullets in Chapter 15). There are a number of reasons for this. It enables the agent to make sensible comparisons. For instance, when selling a stapler, an agent might be asked, 'Why is it so much more expensive than Stapleco's 3200?' If the agent says, 'I don't know anything about that model' (or even worse, 'Who is Stapleco?'), the customer is not going to feel confident in making the purchase. If, on the other hand, the agent can say, 'Theirs does cost less, but ours is better built so it lasts longer, and our special staples come in at half the price', customer confidence will be increased.

Good news story

In tents salesmanship

A customer went into a branch of Millets, a shop specializing in camping and outdoor clothing. She wanted to buy a tent and two air mattresses. The salesman showed her a tent and some mattresses that matched her requirement. The customer pointed out that apparently similar products could be bought from a catalogue shop across the road for less. The Millets salesman said that, quite honestly, she should get her air mattresses from the catalogue shop, because they were identical, but that the tents Millets were selling were proper, waterproof ones, while the catalogue shop's tents were little more than toys, which were only water-resistant. He made the sale (of the tent) and won the admiration of the customer.

In the tent example, the salesman's knowledge of the competitor's products was invaluable. A knee-jerk reaction might be that he had performed badly, because he had sent business elsewhere for the air mattresses. In fact, he had rescued the sale of the tent (worth 20 times as much as an air mattress), which would probably have gone to the catalogue shop otherwise.

The examples above are in sales, but knowledge of other products extends into other areas of customer service. Support staff working on computer software need to have a very wide-ranging awareness of competitors' products, as it is all too easy for interaction between products to cause problems. Agents may be asked about competitors or be required to explain a difference between their services and the opposition's. All agents will benefit from competitor training.

Can you train the customers?

It is worth considering whether your training can extend beyond your agents to your customers. While this doesn't apply to the one-off caller, regular customers may benefit from some types of training, whether it's the ins and outs of your ordering system or how to use your self-help program. This is quite separate from any training customers might receive in your products and services: this is training customers to make best use of your customer service. Whether or not there is any benefit will vary from company to company, but it makes sense at least to consider whether customer training should be part of the package.

12

Roles and empowerment

There has never been a better example of the wider implications of the old 'pay peanuts and get monkeys' adage. If remote customer service staff are to provide positive benefit, they need more reason to buy into the company's direction and objectives. This may be about money, but it is more likely to be about role and the ability to get something done.

Peanuts and monkeys

We all want the best for the lowest price. It's true shopping in the supermarket and it's true when we recruit staff. However, if you think you can take people off the street, pay them a minimum wage and then expect them to represent your company well, you are being unrealistic. There is an element of paying peanuts and getting monkeys here.

What makes the problem more complex is that in the traditional application of the phrase, 'peanuts' simply referred to money. Certainly financial payment comes into it, and agents should be paid well enough to get the calibre of person you require, but you should consider also the nature of the role and how much the agent is given the ability to act on his or her own judgement.

What is an agent?

At the centre of the issue of value, responsibility and empowerment is that of role. How the company sees its agents is fundamental to the role they will actually perform, and the benefits the company can reap from them. This is not a matter of spouting reassuring messages. We've all seen companies that announce in their reports and accounts that 'we value our staff as our most important asset'. If a company has to put such a comment in its report and accounts, either it is stating the obvious or it is attempting propaganda. The acid test, when money is tight, is which assets are disposed of first. If the answer is people, then the statement that 'we value our staff as our most important asset' seems more than a little ironic.

When we're looking at the agent role, we need a real picture of what the agent means to the company. Consider these two job descriptions:

Customer service agent 1

Answers telephone calls when prompted to do so by automated system. Attempts to minimize customer contact time. Refers any decisions involving expenditure to supervisor.

Customer service agent 2

Presents the face of the company to the customer. Ensures that customer gets a good image of the company. Deals with a wide range of problems and challenges. Can take initiative to solve problems within broad guidelines.

These are both possible interpretations of what the agents in your call centre and behind your Web site are about. Of course, they are caricatures, but it is not surprising that we can't get good people for the job if it's seen, both by the agents and by the managers, as being about answering the phone when an automated system tells you to and getting rid of the customer as quickly as possible.

Whether or not it's accepted, that first line in the second description says it all. The agent presents the face of the company to the customer. You can spend as much as you like on advertising and elegant promotional material, it only takes one contact with an agent who hasn't got the right idea of the role and you have lost that customer's business. Of course it's important to keep costs down. But that isn't the primary role of the agent. The agent is there to give a human interface to the company. The better the experience is, the better the company is likely to perform.

How can we help you?

Given a role that is driven by customers, rather than by the call management system, it should be natural that an agent's job involves helping customers. Beware of the difference between a slogan and a role. You can train a parrot to say, 'Hello, my name is Polly, thank you for calling BigCo customer services. How may we help you?' but that's not going to deliver the goods. Too often this is very close to reality. The agent is given those words as a script, but there is no enthusiasm or intent behind them.

The starting point is training and tone, covered in the previous chapter, but there's more to it. Your agents should really want to help customers. Your procedures need to make it practical for them to do so, and your reward scheme should reflect the importance of this to the job.

If you really believe that agents are the key face of the company, and that they should have incentives to give the feeling that they are there to help customers, consider how your reward scheme can reflect this. You should be looking out for these attributes:

- sounds genuine;
- receives letters and e-mails from customers thanking him/her personally;
- is prepared to stay after work to sort out a problem;
- enjoys sorting out problems for people.

As always, there is a need for balance. To be able to help, the agent also needs good time management skills, including a practical application of the 80:20 rule. It isn't always necessary to achieve 100 per cent perfection. Often an 80 per cent solution, which can be achieved in 20 per cent of the time, is enough. Helping people can't be allowed to descend into an absorption in a particular problem that stops other cases being dealt with, but combined with practical time management, helping the customer should be the agent's prime focus.

Flexibility

If agents are to succeed in their complex role, they need to be flexible. They need to be able to assess the situation and respond accordingly, rather than follow a set of fixed rules and procedures. Employers typically resist this vital capability with a lack of trust. We'll look at that more in the next section, but it's not just the employers that get in the way of flexibility.

In the 1990s, many of the strikes that took place were over flexible working. There's no sign of this reaction dying away in the 2000s. When a workforce acts flexibly, it is difficult to have precise job definitions and responsibilities. That makes it hard to have collective bargaining for pay, as each person's job is effectively individual. Traditionally, organized labour has seen this as a bad thing, as it enables the bosses to work the system and keep the workers down.

What's needed is a radically new view on flexibility for agents. It should be seen as an opportunity for them to have a more varied and interesting job, to take more of their own decisions and to have a job that better suits them. To reach that position requires trust from both sides. Employers need to make it clear with their approach to salaries and other benefits that this isn't a way to cut costs. Similarly, flexibility results in employees taking on more responsibility. Organized labour is rightly concerned that this means employees getting the blame when things go wrong. If flexibility is to be central to the role, which is essential if an agent is to function effectively, there needs to be a move from a blame culture to one where lessons are learnt. The only blame should attach to those who repeatedly don't learn the lessons. It comes back to trust.

Horror story

It's not our policy

I bought a computer modem by mail order. It didn't work properly. I rang the manufacturer's help line – after a fair amount of questioning, they confirmed that there was a fault with the modem. So I rang the mail order company's customer service line to find out how to get it replaced. 'Sorry,' they said, 'if there's a fault, you have to send it back to the manufacturer. It's policy.' I pointed out that they have a legal obligation to sell merchantable goods. I didn't want to send it back, so I decided on a refund instead. 'But the policy is that faulty goods have to be sent back to the manufacturer. It's not our problem. We can't do you a refund.' I pointed out their legal obligation again. There was no movement. It was only by talking to a manager that I managed to get any sensible response. The employee was clearly given no leeway in deciding what to do. I won't use them again.

Trust

Trust is central to getting really effective action out of an agent (or for that matter any other member of staff). It is interesting that in a Call Centre Association survey, one of the major issues that staff had was with call monitoring. They felt that the management did not trust them, and that they could not trust management to use recordings appropriately. The disclaimer to the public on the matter of recording usually says that it is for training purposes. Agents know better – it is to reprimand them for not toeing the party line.

A lack of trust has many bad effects. Trust is needed to allow staff to operate flexibly. Trust is needed to give the right customer service at the right time. Take the call monitoring example again. If there was a genuine atmosphere of trust, the only reason for call monitoring would quite genuinely be training. Agents would be happy that they might get some pointers. Tapes could be turned over to agents, who could find the conversations that went wrong, and then play them through with a mentor to see how they could be made better.

Good news story

Semco

Trust is a difficult issue for most companies. Many take the attitude that you just know your employees are out to rip you off, so you can't trust them. In his excellent book *Maverick!* (1994), Ricardo Semler proves that it doesn't have to be that way. Heading up an engineering firm in Brazil, Semler was in the worst possible position to get a culture of trust in his company – blue-collar work, old-fashioned industry, and a unionized, high-inflation country. It hasn't been plain sailing, but Semler has established that trust is possible, and that it provides superb rewards.

The first example of trust was disposing of security checks and searches of employees, but it went much further. Now many of the employees set their own wages, and everyone knows what everyone else is getting. An employee going on a business trip decides how much to spend on a hotel and where to eat. There is no policies and procedures manual. The key to making such a level of trust work is information and communication. Semco puts a huge effort into communicating why there is this atmosphere of trust, what the employee gets out of it, and what the company expects from the employee in return. If it works there, it could work anywhere.

Getting an atmosphere of trust is very important if agents are really to deliver your customer service ideals. It simply isn't possible to give great service when you are treated with suspicion. Note, though, that trust is a matter of culture or atmosphere; it's not something that can be done overnight. You can't just announce that 'we are now a trusting company' and think the job is done. It's a slow, step-by-step process. You will need to loosen the reins on your employees. Show them that this is to their benefit (to start with, they won't trust your motives) as much as yours. Lead them gradually into trust.

At this stage there is usually a doubt. Trust is all very well if all your employees are perfect, but there will be some rotten apples in the barrel, who will welcome your trust culture as an opportunity to rip the company off. It will happen, but the worst case is that a few of your employees (and it had better only be a few, or there's something seriously wrong with your interviewing) will take advantage. Even then, you are likely to find that the solid financial benefits of improved customer service outweigh the losses you make to dishonesty.

The more you do build an atmosphere of trust, the more the employees will be prepared to get involved. The people on the shop floor are the people who are best able to spot things going wrong. With a traditional employer, people are likely to keep quiet about dishonesty. Why should they help a company that doesn't trust them? If, on the other hand, they feel an active part of the company, with buy-in to what the company is trying to do, they are much less likely to turn a blind eye. If they don't report the offender to management or the police, they are likely to sort things out themselves.

This isn't a matter of turning employees into lapdogs of management, as some unions might see it. It's about two-way trust, pure and simple.

Initiative

With an atmosphere of trust in place, the agents can begin to show initiative. This is at the heart of many of the good news stories in this book. An agent has taken the initiative to fix a problem or to make something happen for the customer. A bad agent's viewpoint is that 'it's not my problem'. A good agent is prepared to take the initiative.

Good news story

Gateway

There are plenty of brownie points for US PC manufacturer Gateway in this story.

> Gateway, I have to say, have been very good. You speak to intelligent, inter-ested people who know what they're talking about and assume that you do as well. After the initial contact I dealt with the same man, so I didn't have to go through the whole story each time. He called back when he promised. On the one occasion when he promised to e-mail a patch one evening and it didn't arrive he called the first thing next morning to explain that it had turned out to be unsuitable. They e-mailed drivers, and the latest system BIOS – but when I told them what I'd found they said, 'Well don't apply the patches then; if it ain't broke then don't fix it.'
>
> An earlier experience: when setting the PC up originally I found that the screen was dead. The support person on that occasion said, 'Hold your phone next to the PC, and power it up... Right, your video card needs re-seating; this is how you do it...' Time to fix problem, 10 minutes includ-ing final reboot. I don't know whether the fact that they're based in Ireland makes a difference; one thing that I do appreciate is that their support is on a free line. With another supplier you were paying up to a pound a minute for support.
>
> I must admit that I quite like telephone support. My problem is that when the Bright Young Things come into the office to provide support they see someone who's middle-aged, fat and grey-haired. Trying to persuade them that I might know what I'm talking about can be difficult! When you're invisible they don't pick up on the visual clues, and I do well because I've got a telephone manner that's reasonably friendly and non-aggressive.

Note 'intelligent, interested people', staying in contact with the same person, calling back when promised, explaining delays, on-the-spot action and ingenu-ity, free connection and an unusual positive insight into the benefits of being an invisible customer.

Like the other qualities mentioned in this chapter, initiative is linked into trust. Without trust, agents will not feel capable of taking the initiative. Agents also have to have the sensitivity, intelligence and creativity (see Chapter 16 for more on creativity) to see that there is something wrong and to take appropriate action, but without initiative, the rest is wasted.

Empowerment

Consider the simple matter of taking breaks. No one can work constantly at anything for more than around an hour and a half without serious deterioration of output. It's not just that people want a break, but that the company needs its agents to take breaks to get the best out of them. It is interesting that in the recent Call Centre Association report, flexibility in taking breaks was seen as a desirable change to decrease stress in the workforce. Mechanically enforced break times take control away from agents and introduce unnecessary stress and poor performance.

It's not possible for everyone just to take a break when they want one, or the centre might lose cover. A combination of trust and information is needed. If a group of adults are in the park with their children, they don't need a mechanical system to give individuals a break – they check that there are enough others to cover before popping off for five minutes. Similarly, if agents have access to information about loads and agent availability, there is no reason why they can't take charge of their own break schedule.

Empowerment provides agents with more control, an essential to managing stress and making them better able to be flexible. The word has been overused by management consultants and authors, but is a powerful concept nevertheless. If we maintain all decision-making and power at the centre, the organization will be sluggish, ineffective and unable to respond to a requirement to get something done quickly. Empowerment indicates: 'You are in the front line; it's your place to decide on appropriate action.' Empowerment always requires two inputs, trust and information: trust from both sides that the agent is being given the power to make decisions and carry them through, and sufficient information to make those decisions wisely. The more agents are trapped in a particular way of working, or have to refer a problem to someone else, the worse the customer service becomes. Empowerment is directly connected to quality of service.

Quick tips

Empowerment matters

This senior manager of a large corporate is sure that empowerment is essential for call centres.

Telephone call centres are normally only the contact end of the service – insurance, airline tickets, etc, the real service you're buying, lies outside the call centre. Because it's more impersonal (the server is invisible) I'd make [the agents] customer champions, which means taking the customer's side – make it the job of others in the company to say 'no' when they call the customer back (at the company's expense), and avoid the continuous escalation (I can't decide that – I'll have to refer it to my boss). I can draw an organization chart of my broker from these discussions I've had with them – really empower and give them responsibility.

Taking risks

You can't respond flexibly to changing circumstances without taking risks. All business (all life) involves a degree of risk-taking. We need agents to be able to take risks, which means being able to assess a risk initially. We aren't talking about taking wild risks, but calculated risks: being aware of the possible outcomes of an action and judging that it is sensible to go ahead despite the level of risk.

Once the risk has been taken, the company needs to support its agents. They should not be made scapegoats if something goes wrong. There is a tendency to look for someone to blame that is not helpful in business. Blame is not the issue. Taking risks will inevitably result in some failure; that's simple statistics.

The company's approach to failure should be that of scientists: that it is a valuable learning tool. Failures should be examined, lessons learnt and those involved (particularly agents) made aware of what happened and how such an outcome might be avoided. Calculated risk does need to be part of the agent's armoury, which requires strong support from the centre for the agent's decisions. The company should accept the need for failure and resulting change.

13

Process rules

Remote customer service is about getting the process right, but it's not enough to have good scripts. You need to understand the process customers want to use and be able to support it. In an inflexible environment like IVR or Web site design, this means getting it right by the rules. In a more flexible interaction, it has to be about having guidelines, which are broken as and when it is necessary to give good service.

Get it right

Process is at the heart of the customer satisfaction business. The people on the end of the phone or reading your Web site want to achieve something. The process by which they fulfil that requirement should be driving the design of the system and the service you provide.

It's not as simple as it sounds. If you had only one customer with a single requirement, the problem would be trivial, but in practice every customer's process requirement is subtly different. Luckily, though, there are enough similarities to enable most interactions to be driven by a relatively small number of processes.

Although the customer process is what your whole system is theoretically designed to achieve, the real world is much less helpful. For decades computers have caused as much chaos as they have removed, because it is rare that a computer is flexible enough to fit a human process. Instead, particularly in the early days of computerization, the process had to be modified so that the computer could cope with it.

While computers have moved on a lot, we still allow control of our processes to rest with the computer all too often. For example, I have an account with a telephone bank. This account has two numbers associated with it – a plan number and an account number, each running to 10 digits. I have to quote the plan number whenever I phone up, but as with all the other numbers that apparently define me – national insurance, driver's licence, assorted phone numbers and PIN numbers – it is not a natural thing for me to remember. As we saw in Chapter 9, images and words stick better than numbers. Numbers are used because they're easy for computers, not because they're easy for people. This process is designed, to some extent, around the computer. It's easier to type in a plan number than my name and some other identifier. However, it shows the ease with which a step in the process can be made for the convenience of the company or the computer, rather than the convenience of the customer.

You may well still want to make steps for your convenience – as always there is a trade-off between customer convenience and cost – but it is essential that you are aware that this is what you are doing.

Good news story

Airline tickets

Airline tickets provide a good example of the sort of assumption we make until we analyse the process. Getting tickets seems to be a perfectly logical part of the flight process, but airlines like United Airlines, QANTAS and British Airways have all questioned this. After all, your booking is in the computer system. All the ticket is used for in the flight process is proof of who you are and whether you have flown. If you can accept a computerized proof of flight, then the ticket is purely an ID – and a very poor one at that.

By examining the passenger process from deciding to fly to reaching a destination, airlines have proved the redundant nature of the ticket. A passport (especially in the newer machine-readable form) would be a much better mechanism. If this were adopted, it would simplify the whole process: no picking up tickets and presenting them, just swipe your passport. Technical and (particularly) political diversions have made ticketless travel less common than it could be, but the lesson is there for anyone trying to improve customer service.

The customer process

Customer processes are often drawn up as flow charts or other diagrams, which is helpful in analysing and comparing them. It can help to start by describing the process as a narrative before developing diagrams.

Let's assume, for example, that a customer has a problem with a piece of computer software that isn't working properly with a new computer. A narrative description of the process might go something like this:

> The software won't print. The user looks up printing in the online help; there is no advice. She looks in the documentation; there is no trouble-shooting guide, but there is a phone number for office hours support and a Web site address. It is out of office hours, so she tries the Web site. At the home page there is a button labelled support. She clicks it. The support page offers frequently asked questions and e-mail support. She clicks on the frequently asked questions, and then on printing, but there is nothing about her problem. She clicks on the support button again, and then on e-mail support. Here she fills in a form describing her problem. She gets a confirming auto responder e-mail, and then within 24 hours an e-mail asking for extra information. She replies to that mail. After another 24 hours she gets a mail telling her to try installing a new driver. The mail contains a Web page address. She goes to this and clicks on the button to download a new driver, okays saving to file, and then elects to put the file on her desktop. When the file has downloaded she comes offline and then double-clicks the new file icon. This installs the new driver and tells her to restart her PC. She restarts her PC and tries printing. It works.

Such a description of process may seem tediously detailed, but it is in the detail that we can find what is wrong (and right) with the process. This is only one example. There will be many other processes (for example, she could have tried the telephone number), but usually these can be brought together to form a manageable number of generic processes.

Process walkthrough

Once a first shot at a process like the one above is established, it should be walked through. This is best carried out by having a number of people with experience of different aspects of the business looking through the process description individually. They should look for gaps first, and then consider potential improvements. The group should come together to pool their observations and work on improvements.

In the example above, a possible omission is the detail of how the user looks up printing in online help. There is plenty of room for improvement. Both the online help and the documentation could carry a troubleshooting guide, which would probably include the suggestion of downloading the latest driver. The telephone support could have 24-hour coverage using voice mail or IVR. The Web site could have an interactive troubleshooting guide. The ability to search frequently asked questions would be beneficial, as would the ability to jump straight to e-mail support from any point. If the form had been more specific, the user might not have had to supply extra information, thereby delaying the process by at least a day... and so on.

When walking through and improving a process, you are looking to make the process simpler and more attractive for the customer. Sometimes this is a matter of offering more choice. In a multi-stage process it may involve chopping out some steps entirely. Don't be obsessed with cutting, though – occasionally it will be necessary to add steps to make things simpler.

Translation

When (and I would suggest only when) you understand the customer process, it is reasonable to translate this into the implications for internal processes. You may need a mechanism for escalating or a knowledge base, you may need ways to co-ordinate e-mail, the post and voice contacts, but the value of translating to these processes from the customer process is that it is very clear which is the driver.

This doesn't mean that everything your business needs is directly driven by customer service requirements. From the customer's viewpoint, there is no service advantage to checking the validity of a credit card or categorizing the types of call you receive – these are systems and processes where your company is the beneficiary. However, to ensure that you have above-average customer service, you need to make sure these systems and processes fit around the customer's process rather than the reverse.

Re-engineering

The walkthrough process described above provides incremental change. Often this is valuable. It is probably true, as alleged by John Gall in the book *Systemantics* (1977), that all complex systems that work evolved from a simple system that works. However as a process is continually tinkered with and modified to cope with extra possibilities and new directions, it becomes clumsy and cumbersome. This is the concept behind the weighty structure of business process re-engineering (BPR).

In the business world, BPR has now been largely discredited as doing more harm than good, but it makes sense not just to modify an existing process but to try to design an ideal process from scratch where the existing state is messy. Drive this new process from the customer's viewpoint. This will produce an ideal but impractical process. The skill then is to convert it into a practical process that is still attractive to the customer.

In the sample process above, what the customer would probably like is something like this: the software recognizes that there is a printing problem and fixes its driver so it works properly. This solution is probably not practical. However, it can then be modified a little. Perhaps the help menu could have a repair option that gives the customer the chance to identify a printing problem. The software could then re-load the driver from its disk. If this fails, it could go online and download the latest driver from the Web site.

There is nothing about this that is impossible – most of these elements are available in commercial software – but it is just not currently pulled together in this way. With this entirely practical solution, the customer has her problem solved in minutes rather than two to three days.

Another common process consideration where re-engineering may be relevant is that of processes built around technology or departments instead of customers. You may then find, for instance, that what should be a simple customer-based transaction becomes complicated, as there are quite separate processes in the help-desk system, and the customer database and invoicing systems. If your organization is to serve customers effectively, it may well be necessary to re-engineer these internal processes and systems to reflect customer requirements.

The process starts with the product

An important point that is rarely taken into account when thinking about customer support and customer service is that the process starts with the product. When considering your indirect customer service you have to take the product and its bundled support materials into account. As we saw in Chapter 4, customer exploration is a superbly cost-effective solution if it can be made to work. When looking at the support process, you must try to find ways for satisfying customers that do not involve contacting you. Go back to those instruction books and online help files. Look at any possible mechanisms for automating support. It makes sense for both you and the customer.

Menus that work

Given a good description of the customer process, it should be relatively easy to generate appropriate menus for an IVR system – or scripts for the agents. In practice, there is a problem: the difficulty of keeping customers as a driving force. It's all too easy to fall into a process model that is built around your company and your systems, rather than customers.

This is seen all too clearly in the horror story in Chapter 2. A telephone system that is based around the customer process will divide on the type of customer and what they want to do. What was seen instead was a system where arbitrary internal divisions in the company ('You don't want the hotline, you want sales') are influencing the process. Customers don't care which part of the company is dealing with their requirement. They just want something done. It should not be up to them to deduce the appropriate part of the organization to deal with. The menu customers choose from, whether literally with IVR, or metaphorically, needs to match their needs.

Imagine a real menu that was divided not by customers' needs but by the restaurant's. Instead of splitting up into starters, main courses and puddings, it might have all the foods from one supplier in the same section. If that sounds unlikely, it's worth remembering that some bookshops still have different shelves for different book publishers. The fact that people want a particular type of book or a particular author and don't care who publishes it is beside the point. The bookshop is driving the process from its own requirements rather than the customer's.

Web sites that feel right

Applying the same thinking to Web sites is even more of a breakthrough than applying it to call centres. Too often, Web sites are not designed with the customer process in mind. It's quite obvious that the designers have not sat down and thought 'What does the customer want to do?' and 'How can we make that process as slick as possible?' As far as possible, the key customer processes should be matched by clear buttons on the home page of the site. This must be seen from the customer viewpoint. Too often there is a confusion of 'customer service' and 'FAQ' and 'contact us' and 'downloads' and 'support' and more. These labels aren't necessarily helpful to the customer, who might appreciate much more direct labelling like:

- send us an e-mail;
- download new software drivers;
- get help using your product;
- get help fixing a fault.

A site can't be set up to cover every possible customer requirement. There is still a need for flexible navigation and searching the site, but paths through the site that match customer processes should be seen rather like wizards in computer software – simple step-by-step guides that get a process completed with the minimum of customer effort.

Scripts or guidelines?

We've already considered (see Chapter 6) the benefits of using guidelines and keywords rather than detailed scripts to make an interaction with an agent feel more like a real conversation. There is an apparent clash between this and the desire to fit processes to the customer requirement. If you have a clearly defined process, isn't that, in effect, a script?

In practice, the need to understand processes moves between the detail of scripting and the broad view of guidelines. When investigating a customer process, you will typically go into a lot of detail. This will then translate into a broader set of customer requirements. A detailed script can be built to match these requirements, but then it can be brought up to keyword guidelines for the agents to work from. Following a process does not necessarily mean that you are dealing with rigid scripts, merely that the guidelines should fit with the process.

Taking the plunge

It can be difficult to do anything about processes, particularly under pressure. There is a feeling of 'If it ain't broke, don't fix it.' Any process will age and become less applicable as the world changes, and in many cases the process hasn't been thought through properly (particularly from the customer viewpoint) from the start. When it's broken is too late to fix it – you need to take your processes up to the next level before things go drastically wrong. Site managers should see the implementation of process improvements on a regular basis as one of their significant objectives.

14

Stressed out

Call centre and other support staff are subject to significant stress. A recent report has shown that 98 per cent of call centre staff get at least one stressful call a day, which is no surprise to anyone who has to deal with customers. This chapter looks at helping remote customer staff manage their stress.

A fact of life

Stress is something we hear a lot about in the media. It is a natural part of living. Stress is inherently neither negative nor positive. Good stress gives the edge to excel and propels us into extreme performance when in danger. Bad stress constantly wears away at us, turning our lives into a misery and wrecking health. It may be stress that causes many diseases and loses millions of days at work, but it is also stress that pushes the athlete to achieve his or her best, and stress that makes the difference between moderate and outstanding business performance.

Particular pressures

It's fair to say that anyone involved in customer service is likely to be under more than average stress, but few suffer more than call centre agents. Angry callers are liable to vent their anger on agents. In a 'natural' situation, the agents would respond by either fighting back or running away. Neither possibility is available, and so stress builds up.

To make matters worse, a prime cause of negative stress is being out of control. There is good evidence that it is not necessarily the 'obviously stressful' jobs that result in stress for those undertaking them. For example, an air traffic controller, under a huge amount of pressure at work, is less likely to suffer from stress-related illnesses than a cleaner in the same building. Similarly, a senior manager with hugely complex decisions to make feels less stress than an assembly-line worker.

It seems that self-esteem and being in control are the main factors concerned in putting a worker under stress. The people in the deceptively low-stress jobs have a lot more control over their working life than the cleaner or the assembly-line worker. The low-stress workers may be under huge pressure, but they have a degree of control, and they believe that they and their jobs are valued.

Those who give service to the invisible customer are often at the dangerously stressful end of this spectrum. The job is seen as being of little value. They are often following a scripted process with little opportunity for initiative and intervention. The preceding chapters have shown how it is possible to give more flexibility and control to agents. This approach improves customer service and, as a side benefit, it also decreases stress levels in agents.

It is interesting to see how the stress factors broke down in the Call Centre Association's 1998 survey. Around two-thirds of staff responding felt that they were under significant pressure. From their viewpoint, the big three problems were achieving targets, dealing with difficult customers and the combination of call volume and not having enough time between calls. Some other factors that might seem sources of stress were considered much less significant – complicated calls or not having a competitive-enough product, for example.

The key stressors cannot be considered in isolation. Tight targets and limited time may lead to rushing customers, which is bound in turn to push more callers into the 'difficult' bracket. The need to balance the requirement comes in here. In theory, one of the reasons for targets is to minimize customer wait time and hence improve customer satisfaction, but the pressure to achieve these targets actually irritates customers instead of having the desired effect.

Interestingly, in the same survey, more call centre managers felt their staff were under significant pressure than did the staff themselves, with the same key stress factors.

Whether or not you have taken action to improve your agents' self-esteem, there is likely to be some need for stress management, both in a general sense and in terms of the specific stress factors that come up in surveys.

Stress management

Once you have acknowledged the presence of bad stress, it is possible to do something about it. This isn't a book on stress management – there are several recommended in Appendix 1 – but it is possible to set out a brief view of stress management for agents in this chapter. Stress management shouldn't be seen as a wishy-washy, HR-type issue, but as a practical tool to make sure that your agents deliver their best and stay at the job. As a side effect, it will also make life better for them.

Stress management is inevitably more pragmatic than idealistic. The most effective approach is to remove the source of stress before it can do any damage (or at least to limit the damage). For example, many people regard the daily drive to work as a necessary evil. It does cause stress, but 'there's nothing we can do about it, so we've got to suffer'. The constraint, though, is entirely down to the person suffering the stress. It is, in fact, possible to do away with this stressor. You could:

- take a different route;
- use public transport;
- get a bike or motorbike;
- car share and let someone else do the driving;
- work from home;
- move house;
- change your job.

It might seem that some of these choices are rather extreme to overcome an irritating drive to work, but the point is that it is quite possible to change the circumstances, and the choice is yours. What's more, if commuting to work really is a painful exercise that takes away hours of your life every week, maybe it is worth resorting to a drastic solution to improve your quality of life.

Sometimes, though, it is genuinely impossible to remove the stressor, or the alternatives are even less desirable than the present state. In such circumstances, stress management takes a different approach. Where you can't remove the stressor, you can take action to mitigate the impact it has. This might take the form of physical action to reduce stress – anything from massage to simple breathing exercises – or mental and spiritual techniques to reduce the impact of stress on your life. Whichever approach or combination of approaches you take, it is always possible to do something about negative stress. For example, if you decide despite all the alternatives that you are really stuck with the same old daily drive into work, just getting a really interesting set of book tapes – a mix of fiction and non-fiction – can do a lot to take away the strain.

Removing stressors

Removing the stressor entirely is in some senses the ideal. After all, there is no need to worry about stress if there is nothing causing it. Often, taking this approach to stress management is a matter of seeing how you can do things differently. In the commuting example, we have already seen how you might be able to get to work a different way, or even turn the problem on its head and get the work to come to you. Under such circumstances, you have taken away the stressor. Commuting is still a problem – but not for you any more.

Some aspects of the call centre and Web service jobs are immovable. It doesn't matter how many stickers you put up saying 'This job would be great if it wasn't for the customers', they aren't going to go away. None the less, there are some stressors that those dealing with invisible customers can avoid or mitigate. What they are will vary from environment to environment, but here are a few suggestions.

Stress often comes from your working environment. Are there ways to make this more pleasant and personal? Anything from a comfy chair to personal pictures and enough soundproofing to avoid leaks from other agents might help. Look too at the nature of the job allocation mechanisms. There's nothing wrong with these being used to keep the flow going, or even to introduce competition, but they should not feel threatening or inhuman. Make sure the technology is up to the job. If you are well motivated, there is nothing worse than finding the tools you have been given simply don't deliver. Saving money by buying cheap and nasty PCs or not providing effective phone technology is a false economy.

In the Call Centre Association's 1998 survey, the most frequently listed approaches to relieving stress echo these suggestions. 'Developing a relaxed and friendly atmosphere', 'creating team spirit', 'employing more staff' and 'training' came top, while it was felt that allowing more time for paperwork, flexibility in breaks and improved communication were the areas that most needed to be improved on.

Finally, there's the catch-all. Angry contacts tend to be in response to poor customer service. If you can improve customer service across the board, you will reduce the number of angry calls you get, which means a reduction in stress as well. This is just another reason for making sure you do something about customer service. From the agent's viewpoint, it isn't just a matter of improving company profitability (and hence keeping a job), but of improving health.

Physical relief

Physical relief employs physical means to manage stress. The most direct means of physical relief is the use of drugs, but in most instances this is not necessary. Stimulants (like alcohol, caffeine-bearing drinks or cigarettes) make stress worse, even though most of us tend to resort to them as a counter to stress. That's not to say that there's anything wrong with settling down with a glass of wine and a book after work – quite the reverse in most cases – but the wine alone will not help. What is effective is the overall unwinding process of which the wine is a psychological positive part even though it is itself physiologically negative. However, there is much more to physical relief than the chemical.

The agent's job provides a particularly good example of the need for a physical counter to stress. There has never been a time when people have led such sedentary lives as they do now, and agents tend to go through most of their stressful interactions slumped in a chair. Most people need more exercise, both to counter the chemical output of stress and to get healthier and hence better able to cope with the effects of stress. As far as agents are concerned, it should be made easier for them to get up and walk around while doing their job. Do their headsets allow this? More importantly, finding ways to bring mild aerobic exercise into the day (a 20-minute burst of fast walking is probably enough) can help a lot.

Action station

Breathing better

It's a self-evident truth that breathing is a good thing – but there's breathing and there's breathing. Firstly, as all singers know, there are two types of breathing: with the chest muscles and with the diaphragm. The latter is more controlled and gives you a much deeper breath, yet it tends to be underused, particularly by those under stress. This is unfortunate, as long, slow diaphragmatic breathing naturally reduces stress levels and makes you better able to cope with a problem.

First, try to feel that diaphragmatic breathing. Stand up, straight but not tense. Take a deep breath and hold it for a second. Your chest will rise. Now try to keep your chest in the 'up position' while breathing in and out. You should feel a tensing and relaxing around the stomach area. Rest a hand gently on your stomach to feel it in action.

Now lie on the floor or sit comfortably in a chair. Close your eyes. Begin to breathe regularly: count up to five (in your head!) as you breathe in through your nose. Hold it for a second, and then breathe out through your mouth, again counting to five. Rest a hand on your stomach. Don't consciously force your rib cage to stay up now, but concentrate on movement of the diaphragm. Your stomach should gently rise as you breathe in and fall as you breathe out.

This breathing exercise can help relieve stress invisibly in almost any environment.

Other more indirect forms of physical relief from stress like massage and aromatherapy can be provided directly or enabled by giving your staff easy access to appropriate treatment or training. It isn't essential to build a gym in the basement, or to provide aromatherapy oils in the staff canteen, but giving some thought to stress relief can make a lot of difference.

Mental and spiritual relief

Probably the hardest part of stress management to deal with in the business environment is the mental and spiritual side. Just giving people an opportunity to do something completely different for a few minutes can make a lot of difference to the amount of stress they suffer. Combine this with a degree of self-determination in what they are doing when, and the mental side of stress control kicks in strongly.

Of course, as in any production-line environment, it is easy to argue against the practicality of self-determination in the call centre. 'We can't have people doing what they want when they want, or there would be no one to answer the phones' goes the argument. But this is an argument that results in a degrading loss of humanity, including for example having to ask permission from a computer before being allowed to go to the toilet. It is entirely possible to combine a lot of self-management with such environments, provided the information flows are appropriate. If the staff have the right motivation and the right information, they will make sure that the calls get covered – but they are rarely given such support.

As with physical possibilities like breathing exercises, it is also possible to give your staff a mental armoury of techniques they can use quickly when under pressure to help relieve the problem. We should not overlook the spiritual dimension in its broadest sense of looking for something beyond the mundane. Humankind is always searching for meaning and context for what happens. If you can help with this spiritual pursuit – which may simply amount to making sure that those with religious beliefs can take the appropriate days off work or encouraging staff to take the time to go beyond the obvious drivers of money and success to find what it is that really fulfils them – you can also help keep stress in check.

Action station

Life, the universe and everything

One of the main motivations for exploring the spiritual dimension of stress management is the realization that money and property aren't everything. Most of us want to be comfortable, and many would like to be rich, but the consistent story from those who have it all in material terms is that it isn't enough.

Spend a few minutes thinking about the end of your life. This isn't morbid; it's something we know is going to happen. What would you like to look back on and feel happy about? There will probably be elements of money and possessions, but get a full picture. Try to get a feel for the balance.

With this picture in mind, look at your activities. Could you include more that doesn't involve wealth and possessions? Can you achieve a better balance, and hence reduce the feeling that something is missing from your life? Try to come up with a couple of possible directions that you can work on over the next few months.

Some miss out by pursuing the material at the expense of everything else: the people who miss out on family life to concentrate on their career; the people for whom accumulating more and more money is the only driver; the people who think having fun (or lunch) is for wimps – they just don't have time for it. This exercise is about you, the very core of what you are and the reasons behind it. Don't skip over it if you think it sounds too wishy-washy; it is entirely relevant.

Particularly as you reach mid-life, you may consider the discomfort of all your achievements being centred around earning money and accumulating possessions a heavy burden. Aiming for a more balanced life will help iron out these stresses.

It's often the case with physical stress relief that it can be imposed from the outside, but for mental and spiritual relief staff need to be in the right frame of mind to engage in stress management themselves. Initially this may well seem to them like yet another management fad, but it is important that there is appropriate training and reading available to help staff make the decision to manage stress for themselves.

DIY or expert

A lot of stress management can be undertaken in a do-it-yourself fashion, either by agents themselves or by their managers or human resources personnel. Usually the best person to do it is the individual, and a number of the books in Appendix 1 focus very much on this approach. Occasionally, however, it is sensible to bring in an expert.

One problem with stress is that it is not a simple state, but a mixture of the physical and the mental both in origins and symptoms. This means that it is not always easy to separate symptoms – ranging from a damaged back to clinical depression – into those that indicate stress and those caused by a physical illness. If there is any doubt, it is important that professional medical help be sought to make sure exactly what is happening.

Even if you know you are dealing with stress, expert help can be useful. Although getting a massage from a friend can be very effective, a professional will often be able to provide a more searching and relaxing treatment. Similarly, talking through stresses with a friend can help, but an analyst may be able to give more practical suggestions. However, for most people an analyst is entirely unnecessary in helping manage everyday stress.

Control and self-esteem

At the heart of much stress management is the realization of the importance to coping with potential stressors of being in control and having good self-esteem. The way that agents are managed in your company will have a major impact on these factors. We saw in Chapter 12 how giving agents the ability to take appropriate risks and empowering them to make decisions and to take action provides significant benefit to the customer service that can be provided in a changing, uncertain world. Almost as a side effect, such empowerment also decreases employee stress by improving the level of control an individual has over his or her day-to-day activities, and boosting self-esteem.

While stress management might not seem enough benefit in its own right (although reduction in employee absenteeism and improved performance and productivity are likely to result from better stress management), there is real synergy of advantage when agents are trusted and given the ability to make realistic decisions. Business guru Tom Peters has been very scathing about synergy (the concept that the whole can be more than the sum of the parts), but he was thinking about outdated monolithic organizations that imagined there was advantage to be gained from piling everything into a single company. A similar misguided view of synergy is the concept of central purchasing, so beautifully pilloried by Scott Adams in the Dilbert cartoons. All such 'synergy' does is put barriers in the way of getting things done, and make things more expensive for an individual in return for apparent 'group savings'. However, there is a real and positive synergy, where giving staff trust and the ability to act provides *both* great customer service *and* improved stress management.

What can the company do?

If, as I have suggested, stress management is often best instigated by the individual, is there anything that your company can sensibly do to help agents with stress problems? In fact, there is plenty. It all begins with a recognition that stress exists, and that suffering from stress is a real problem both for the agent and for the company. Following on, there is a role for both education and support to help agents manage their stress.

Quick tips

Helping with stress management

- Recognize that being an agent is a stressful job.
- Enable your agents to have more control of their day-to-day actions.
- Emphasize the value of the agents to the company – not just with words but results.
- Provide simple stress management books like this author's *Instant Stress Management* (2000) for your staff.

- Make it easy to get appropriate medical assistance to clarify symptoms.
- Help staff to take exercise by providing facilities or easy access.
- Help staff to relax by having places to get away from it all.

Note, by the way, that this is not something the company should parcel up and hand over to human resources to fix. Remember the importance of self-worth to stress management. The message managers give when they hand a problem over to HR is that it isn't really important to the running of the company. Taking positive steps towards helping agents deal with stress should be part of the line manager's role.

15

Technology triumphs

The very existence of remote customer service implies some contribution of technology to the relationship, but this chapter looks at the ways technology can support your agents to provide a better experience for the customer.

You can't do without it

We have already seen the impact of interactive voice response (IVR) and the potential for natural language IVR, but technology is present throughout the interaction with the remote customer. In a call centre it starts with the very mechanics of the call. The basic telephone is so strongly embedded in our society that we almost forget that it is technology. Once the call reaches the centre it will be distributed by technology. Agents may be given appropriate information, and actions will be taken – all involving technology.

For the Web site, dependent as it is on remarkably new developments, the importance of the technology is more obvious. The Web did not really have commercial applications before around 1996. No technology has become so embedded in society so quickly as the Internet. However the requirement goes beyond the relatively trivial matters of HTTP (laying out pages) and building a Web site. Technology may be involved in the sort of personalization described in Chapter 9, and in linking Web sites with other information and means of communication, from call-me-back buttons to Web phones.

Databasics

At the heart of customer support technology is the database. This is (in computing terms) an old and well-understood technology. In fact, databases predate computers. A set of record cards with standard sets of information on each line, or an address book, is a database. A database consists of a set of identically formatted records, each containing several pieces of information (fields).

Perhaps the biggest contribution the computer has made to information storage is the concept of relational databases. In a conventional set of record cards (in computing parlance, a flat file database), each card holds the full set of information for that record. Say you had cards with details about customers, and 20 of those customers worked for BigCo. If BigCo moved to a new office block, you would have to change the address on each of those 20 cards. A relational database takes such shared information and, instead of reproducing it as many times as is required, just holds it once. In the BigCo example, the 20 cards would now only say that the customer worked at BigCo, and a separate, single company card would give BigCo's address. This is fiddly on paper, but with a computer's speed it is possible to present the information as if it were held on each card (record), while actually holding it in one place.

The central database for the site is the customer database. This holds as much information as possible about the customer, and will ideally be tapped into by any secondary systems, maintaining this 'relational' approach. If, for instance, customers' telephone numbers are recorded in the database, then an incoming call can have its number checked against that database to attempt to identify the caller. There may be other physical databases, but the ease with which the IT systems regard the collection of databases as a single entity will show how good (or not) those systems are.

Handing out calls

Once upon a time, all switchboards had operators. To ring from one place to another involved speaking to your local operator who would set up a long-distance connection, and then dealing with the operator at the end of that connection to reach your actual destination. Now we accept direct dialling as the norm to connect to anywhere in the world. Similarly, while it is possible for all incoming calls to a company to be routed through a person, the usual approach for a call centre is the automatic call distributor or ACD.

At the most basic, the role of the ACD is to act as a buffer and connector between incoming callers and agents. When calls come in, the ACD switches them to available agents. If none is available, it is down to the ACD to put callers in a queue, let them know what is happening and switch them to an agent when one becomes available. This process is often combined with IVR to get extra information about callers while they are waiting, and sometimes to influence the final routing. The features of a modern ACD can be very broad. They might:

- have a complex structure of responses, depending on the nature of the call, the time of day, the length of the queue and other factors;
- use caller ID (also known as caller line identifier, caller display and automatic number identification) to identify the caller, after which the ACD can either route this number with the call to the agent, or use the information to select an appropriate agent or action;
- use the number the caller dialled to choose different options;
- route calls to off-site teleworking agents;
- route faxes as well as voice calls;
- provide voice mail, so that the caller can leave a message if the agent isn't available;
- override an existing call that an agent is dealing with, for example if the new call is an emergency;
- interact with Web sites to call an individual back automatically when an agent is available;
- collate statistics on waiting time, number of callers, etc and route these to the agent's screen.

Telephone tricks

All telephone technology today involves computers, but until recently the basic exchange functions (the 'switch') and the ACD came from telecommunications companies, while network and desktop computers came from computer companies. These two technologies, practically very similar, were not easy to connect together, as computer engineers would not talk to telecommunications engineers (regarding them as old-fashioned), while telecommunications specialists were equally uncomfortable with computer engineers (regarding them as upstarts). Each environment developed its own standards, and there was a degree of chaos.

Latterly, however, telecommunications engineers have recognized that computer engineers have won the battle. The sheer volume of computers meant that the cheapest way to build switch and ACD hardware was to make use of computer components. The opportunity opened up to make it easier for the two to get together, and computer telephony integration (CTI) was born.

Although technically CTI covers every aspect of computers and telephony working together, from a humble desktop modem to the latest digital switch, in practice it is most often used to refer to the interaction between switches, ACDs and agents' desktop computers. Thanks to CTI, if an incoming call carries caller ID information, that information can be passed to the agent's computer. This can then look up the caller in a contact database and, if found, pop up the caller's details and history on the screen.

This is the ideal position. I remember being at a presentation on CTI a few years ago. When I asked a question about dealing with people whose numbers don't show up on caller ID, a delegate behind me tapped me on the shoulder. 'Do you mean that the system I've just paid for won't identify all my customers?' he asked, ashen-faced. His vendor had misled him. In fact anything between 10 and 90 per cent of incoming calls can be without caller ID information.

Some of this is down to technical limitations. Older analogue mobile phones don't support caller ID. Many call boxes and international calls don't provide caller ID information. Business customers often present problems, as all but the most modern (and expensive) private exchanges are incapable of giving out a direct-line number. This being the case, the exchange can either give the switchboard number or mark the caller ID as unobtainable. Older exchanges don't support caller ID. Then there are the withholders. Because of pressure from civil liberties groups, anyone can withhold caller ID, either on an individual call-by-call basis or for all calls from a particular line. The most common businesses withholding the information are telephone sales organizations, which don't want their agents rung back, but individuals can and do also withhold.

Making use of caller ID is not the only function of CTI, though. Interaction between the ACD and the computer network means that calls can be routed to the most appropriate agent in terms of workload or expertise. CTI can also provide the mechanism for customer call-backs, putting customers into the outgoing calling lists of agents. This is a small part of the way CTI can make it practical to have agents handling a mix of incoming and outgoing calls. Such hybrid agents are particularly valuable when the peaks of ingoing and outgoing work are at different times.

Another role for CTI is to provide a friendly interface for telephony. Donald Norman, in *The Psychology of Everyday Things* (1988), rightly argues that the telephone keypad is very poorly designed for the extended functionality of modern telephony. Who can remember that (say) *89*1234# is the code to transfer a call to extension 1234? By putting all the controls of the telephony on agents' screens, they can pick numbers off and dial them, or use all the advanced functions of the exchange without remembering obscure codes.

An interesting possibility that CTI raises is the ability to extend the call centre into an informal network through most of the company. Conventional ACD is usually limited to the call centre itself. With proper CTI support, it is possible to switch a call and associated information, or perhaps just an e-mail requiring a call-back, through to almost anyone in the company. This is unlikely to replace front-line agents, but can provide valuable back-up where a technical specialist or someone with particular line functionality (for example, a legal specialist) is needed to take over a contact.

Finally, and perhaps most importantly as other communication media than the telephone become more and more crucial, CTI enables the integration of all communication media to a single point of access. Once upon a time, agents had to walk around the room using separate fax machine, telex (remember telex?), phone, typewriter and e-mail terminal. Now the whole can be integrated, allowing a balance to be made between handling voice calls and other media. Even paper mail can be scanned on entry to the company and integrated into the system. Where this is achieved, not only do agents get a better mix and overview of their communications, but also it is much harder for customers to 'fall through the cracks', as the requirement to do something will be in the same action list whatever the source of the communication.

Web wonders

The Web is a strange contrast – in one sense it is pure technology, yet it is the content that makes or breaks a Web site, not the fancy gizmos. Hi-tech, state-of-the-art sites may attract those who are out simply to enjoy the experience of surfing, but they can put off new customers, or existing customers looking for support. The best Web technologies are subtle, as with the sort of personalization discussed in Chapter 9.

Behind personalization, a key Web technology is the ability to link Web pages to a database. This works two ways, both in presenting data that comes from a database on a Web page and also in linking knowledge of who is online with your customer database. Linking to existing systems is the big difference between an ordinary business page and an effective corporate page aimed at bringing Web usage into the wider customer interface. For example, when a customer clicks on a 'call-me-back' button, the response should link into the same CTI system that handles calls at the call centre.

One special development that is becoming more practical as customers get faster connection to the Web is IP telephony. It is possible to have a speech contact with the customer across the Internet. This has the advantage of seeming more tightly integrated with the Web site – you don't use a separate telephone – and costing your company nothing extra, wherever in the world the customer is. The disadvantage of IP telephony is that the customer has to have a microphone and speakers attached to his or her PC – not common in a business environment – and the quality of sound is not up to that of a conventional phone.

As technology advances, and customers move beyond simple modems and telephone lines to connect to the Web, IP telephony can move on to using video connections – popping up a window on the Web page where customers can see the agent they are speaking to. Failing that, there is an intermediate facility that is possible: show and tell. The agent talks to customers and actively guides them through a series of Web pages, using the Web as an adjunct to the conversation. Show and tell is particularly effective for saving a failing transaction, by showing customers aspects of the product that they are not aware of, or in encouraging cross-selling and up-selling. It is the nearest method possible with remote customers to sitting next to them and leading them through sales literature, or helping them to fill in a complex form.

There is one aspect of the Web in this technology role that doesn't require anything very hi-tech. We have looked elsewhere at the basics of making a Web site usable by your customers. One way to ensure that the right information is easy to reach is to use the same Web site as both the system that supports your agents and the public site. There will usually have to be add-on databases of proprietary and personal information, but for the most part it makes a lot of sense. Why wouldn't you want your customers to be able to access the same rich knowledge base as your agents? Making the system cover both will ensure that the most appropriate information is readily available from the Web site. There are, however, two potential problems with this approach. The first is covering your backs and the second is the idiot-versus-expert debate.

As far as the first goes, there is a traditional corporate fiction that your competitors can never do anything decent, and your company never makes a mistake. It's not unlike politics, where opposing parties are rarely able to compliment each other's actions and ideas, no matter how close together they actually are. However, a good customer service team need to know your products, warts and all. If the Web site covers all the flaws in your system, it won't be bad for business. The stance that your products are perfect fools no one, least of all your customers. Salespeople are given 'silver bullets' that rip apart the opposition's products without having any idea of the strengths of those products. When they have to deal with informed customers, who do know both products, they are at a real disadvantage. Similarly, a Web site that pretends there's nothing wrong with your products will only fool people briefly. After that it will irritate. It is much better if the public can see that you recognize flaws in your products and are working on improvements. Of course this last part requires you to listen when customers ask for improvements, but you should be doing that anyway.

There is a more delicate balance in the idiot-versus-expert debate. This was seen in fine detail in developments in airline check-in during the 1980s. Most airlines used large mainframe computer systems, dating back to the 1960s and 70s to support their check-in. This involved typing obscure text commands to a cursor with no menus or other form of help – you had to know what you were doing. By the late 80s, however, the advent of PCs meant that it was possible to put a friendly face on the check-in system. Several airlines developed such 'front-end' systems. The idea was that the same system could be used to provide check-in facilities for anyone from a customer using a touch screen, to an inexperienced temporary agent, to long-term experienced staff.

The initial results were poor. Although the existing mainframe systems were hard to use, the condensed command language that the agents were well trained in made it possible to undertake requests much more quickly than by working through a series of menus. In the end a compromise was reached, with check-in staff using a front end that still let them use their complex commands but in a multi-windowed system, while the easy-to-use system for direct access by customers was made even simpler.

In the airline example it was not practical to merge the expert and idiot systems, as the staff were often executing complex commands. However, the call centre example is significantly different. In the call centre example, agents more often look up information, a process that needn't be much more complex than that undertaken by a typical Web user. What's more, just as a popular commercial Web site like Amazon has both a 'simple' search box in which you can type practically anything and also an in-depth search facility where the user types very specific requirements into different boxes, so it would be simple to have an agent-only search facility giving much more control than is available to the public. The idiot-versus-expert problem is not an argument against customers and agents using the same site.

Adopting a single site isn't going to be an overnight decision. Many companies are still uncomfortable with sharing so much information with their customers (and by implication, their competitors). But as the understanding that trust is at the centre of effective business relationships extends, we are likely to see more and more use of this very effective approach to minimizing the need to maintain two parallel systems, and reducing the systems training needed for agents.

16

Driven change

If there's one certainty in this fast-changing environment, it is that you can't rest on your laurels. This chapter looks at managing constant improvement in customer service facilities, by watching the opposition, watching technology and listening to the customer.

Sit back and fail

Lewis Carroll had a remarkable appreciation of the realities of life. His description in *Through the Looking Glass* of how it is necessary to run to stay in the same place has been used so much that it verges on a cliché, yet it has never been more true and relevant. The increase in pace of modern business, especially around the customer service area, continues. The need for change, the need to be constantly developing products and services, the need constantly to improve customer service is not something you can ignore. Complacency inevitably results in failure.

If your company is doing well, you might not see that these strictures apply. However, there is no opportunity to sit back and enjoy the results of your labours. The pressure is still on, and staying at the top will require more than just more of the same. Despite this, it's not a negative story. Change might be driven by the environment, but that doesn't mean that it has to be depressing. It just has to be seen as part of everyday business life, not something special to be considered when you do a spot of strategic planning.

Learn from the opposition

One of your principal drivers for change has to be your competitors. What hasn't sunk in for some companies who depend on invisible customers is the frightening flexibility of the environment. When a supermarket chain decides to change its look, it takes months to implement the change fully. A Web site can be totally transformed overnight, wrong-footing the competition. Take online bookstore Amazon. The US store has continually added new product lines. Recently, the UK store followed suit, adding CDs to the books. This change happened overnight, without warning. Every other UK bookshop and CD shop is suddenly at a disadvantage, because customers can make use of all Amazon's personalization, like 1-Click shopping, across both product lines.

Keeping on top of what competitors are doing is essential. If you are in the Web selling business you ought to be checking out your key competitors daily to keep track of their changes. You also need to be able to take a sideways look at competition. It should have been obvious to UK CD shops for quite a while that Amazon.co.uk would move in that direction, so Amazon should have been on their list.

Learning from the opposition goes beyond keeping up, though. To be truly competitive, a company needs to go one better. Don't just copy the opposition, but improve on it. In part this can be done by combining your own ideas with the best of theirs – but it also helps to watch other sites that are completely unconnected to your own. An insurance company might pick up a great idea from a car site. As well as daily monitoring of your competitors, it's a good idea to have a trawl of some of the hot new sites and see what is being provided.

Similarly, call centres can't rest on their laurels. If you haven't got someone regularly ringing up your competitors asking for information and getting help with problems with their products, you aren't doing your job. If you are left with a creaky old IVR system with seven layers of menus and your main competitor has brought in a natural language system where customers can get what they want in a single request, you are in trouble unless you find out early and do something about it.

The most important message here is to avoid smugness. However good you are, there will be companies out there that come up with ideas that you don't. There will be new concepts that should make you want to change. To believe your own cheerleading about being the best, and hence ignore what everyone else is doing, is potentially fatal.

Measurement and monitoring

A key to effective change is measurement and monitoring. We've already seen how monitoring the opposition is an important part of the requirement. You also need to monitor yourself. With personalization, a Web site is capable of very detailed monitoring of customer behaviour. At call centres, call monitoring is the norm. However, because of a lack of trust, it currently causes bad feeling amongst agents, as it is seen as spying on them. Call monitoring is necessary but, as discussed in Chapter 12, it is essential that work is done with agents to make sure that call monitoring is used as tool to help individuals improve, not as a trap to catch them out.

Measurement in call centres can also be something of a problem. Traditionally, measures were based on throughput. Performance was effectively considered solely on the rate at which agents or centres handled calls and the number of calls lost. This approach is fatal for customer service. What is needed is an approach more like that of the balanced scorecard developed by Robert Kaplan and David Norton, first discussed in the *Harvard Business Review*.

This is a very simple, yet powerful, concept. As initially conceived, the scorecard was applied to business performance, where financial results had traditionally been the only measure. Kaplan and Norton argued that the information revolution had forced a need for a wider base of measurement. Before business became the chaotic, unpredictable beast it is today, it didn't really matter too much what you measured. Now, though, it's possible to have your customers taken away by a totally unexpected competitor. You need a much better feel of what's happening to your company.

Kaplan and Norton suggested using a balanced scorecard of indicators from four aspects of the company – finance, internal business processes, learning and growth, and the customer. It's not a matter of choosing between financial measures and customer service – they're equally important. The idea is to pull these measures together to get an overall picture of the state of the business. Exactly what the measures are will vary from business to business. Kaplan and Norton suggest asking questions about each area so as to be able to identify the measures, questions like 'To succeed financially, how do we need to look to our shareholders?' and 'To achieve our vision, how should we appear to our customers?'

For the call centre or Web site, the measures will be slightly different from those of the whole business. For example, the finance measures may well incorporate call handling times, but there is still the need for balance across the card. (See Appendix 1 for further reading on the balanced scorecard.)

Technology hints

As well as watching your competitors and yourself, you need to keep an eye on technology. Sometimes developments are driven by the business, but sometimes change comes from the technology itself. No one in business said 'We want the World Wide Web' – the technology came first, and then the business imperative. In dealing with the invisible customer you are inevitably dependent on technology. Because of this, it is sensible to maintain a watching brief on that technology as well as the current applications.

In part this can be done by subscribing to technology magazines (both news-stand and trade), but increasingly the Web can help. Visit vendors' sites to see what they are up to. Use the Web sites of technology magazine publishers to get less biased information. Web addresses come and go, but at the time of writing it is worth using these:

- Ziff Davies (US) – http://www.zdnet.com
- VNU (UK) – http://www.vnunet.com

Another useful source is press releases. There are at least two online press information services that provide information in advance of most magazines. There is also Silicon, which provides both articles and videos as well as press information. See:

- The Source – http://thesource.dwpub.com
- NewsDesk – http://www.newsdesk.co.uk
- Silicon – http://www.silicon.com

Listening to the customer

It seems obvious that a major driver for change should be your customers. If you aren't listening to what they want, if you aren't taking note of their comments on your services, you are ignoring one of the most significant sources of information you have. Most companies think they're good at listening to their customers. Unfortunately, many companies are actually hopeless at this task.

A major stumbling block for call centres and Web sites is the attitude of agents to comments from customers. No one likes being criticized, and it is all too easy to take customers' suggestions as criticism. The trouble is, this has a two-fold negative effect. Suggestions that may have been valuable to the company are ignored, and customers may well pick up the negative vibrations and lose faith in the company.

Take the example of the online insurance company highlighted in Chapter 11. In the example, I used the e-mail I received in reply to pointing out a flaw with their service. It is defensive, and shows no sign of taking the comment on board. Before sending the e-mail, I had pointed out the problem to the agent at the call centre. Her reply was something like 'Oh, yeah, we'll have to do something about that', said in a tone that made it clear that she had no intention of passing the information on, and that I was wasting her time. This is not a good image to give the company.

To support the process of gaining comments from your customers, agents (and Web sites) should have easy access to a means of directing comments to someone who can do something about them – not someone who will note them down and forget them, but someone who is capable of taking action if necessary. Customers are a supremely valuable source of ideas for change that should not be lost. They may not always understand, or may have ideas that can't be implemented, but to ignore all customer suggestions is to throw away the baby with the bath water.

A final step, which doesn't particularly help the change process but is important for keeping up levels of customer satisfaction, is to acknowledge suggestions and let customers know what is happening and why. Pouring suggestions into a black hole is discouraging. If customers ask you to make a change, you are much more likely to keep them if you get back to them, thanking them for suggestions, letting them know when their ideas are being implemented or why they can't be. Too few companies do so.

Listening to your staff

If customers are ideally placed to say what could be changed about your company, your products and your services, then so are your agents and other customer contact staff. It's true that they will see the company from a different viewpoint from that of customers, but their presence at the sharp end of the business gives them a powerful insight that you can't afford to ignore. What's more, your customer contact staff often have a better idea of what the competition is up to than the rest of the company. Make use of that resource.

Horror story

By the rule book

Amazon, the online bookseller, has the best-subscribed affiliate programme in the business. As we saw in Chapter 3, such schemes extend your Web customer service across other people's sites. In exchange for this exposure, the site owner is offered some form of commission on sales made from the site.

Unlike many others that run affiliate schemes, Amazon has a rule that affiliates can't buy for themselves. This is a dubious concept. After all, most book site owners are likely to be book enthusiasts, and will buy a lot given the chance. All normal bookshops give their staff much larger discounts than the commission that affiliates receive. If Amazon makes money out of sales from affiliates (why have them otherwise?), it will make money out of self-sales.

Whether or not Amazon should allow affiliates to buy is a moot point. However, what is certainly true is that Amazon mishandled their response to affiliates requesting that the ban be lifted. Their replies simply quoted their rules. This demonstrates that they were not listening to the affiliates, who are effectively their salespeople. The affiliates knew the rules, otherwise they wouldn't have asked for a change. What they wanted to know was why it wasn't possible to change the rules (or even better to hear when they would be changed), something that Amazon did not attempt to answer.

When dealing with your staff, listen to their suggestions. Don't reject them just because 'that's the way we do things round here' – consider making changes where they seem sensible. If you don't, explain why it's not a good idea, don't quote the rule book.

The Amazon affiliates example shows how you have to consider the bigger picture – not just your own agents, but everyone in the chain. By not listening and worse still by making it obvious that you aren't interested in listening, you can undermine your agents and other customer contact staff and miss out on real opportunities for improvement.

Being creative

At the core of managing to keep on top of driven change is creativity. Without creativity at the heart of your company you are not going to be able to manage in the incredibly fast-paced, ever-changing world of modern business. Companies who rely on the invisible customer are at the leading edge of that business wave, and as such they are more in need of creativity than practically any other.

We tend to think of creativity as something you either have or don't have. In fact it is something that can be brought out by using well-established techniques. These techniques push individuals in new directions and into new modes of thought, enabling them to solve problems and come up with new ideas that would not have been otherwise possible. This isn't the book to go into enhancing your company's or your personal creativity (see Appendix 1 for some recommendations), but it is important that creativity is seen as one of the main requirements in coping with driven change, and that action is taken to bring creativity to the company as a whole and to agents in particular.

The invisible agenda

This final chapter pulls together the different requirements of the invisible customer into a practical agenda for taking on or improving remote customer service.

The agenda

This book has worked through a wide range of considerations relevant to serving the invisible customer better. The purpose of this chapter is to bring these together in an agenda for change. How you implement change in your own company depends on the company and who you are. Agents can apply the concepts at a personal level; managers will be looking to make wider changes. In either case, the opportunity is there to make your company stand out with the quality of its service to the remote customer. And in the long term, this can be a matter of survival.

Putting the customer first

Call centres and the Web are about communication with customers, and these parts of the organization should be primarily driven by customer requirements. In practice, all too often it is the needs of the company that come first. There has to be some consideration of company needs. Costs have to be controlled. Sales have to be made. How customers perceive the company as a result of your actions, and the quality of customer service you give, should also be constantly in the mind of those staffing and managing call centres and Web service centres. There is no room for complacency. Customers are rarely given the level of consideration needed. It's time to put them first.

Pulling together the media

Central to the agenda from a management viewpoint is the need to pull together the different communications media through which customers might contact your company. It isn't good enough any more to have separate handling of letters, e-mails, the call centre and the Web site. Integrated customer information and integrated handling are essential both to give the customer the best service and to give that small-company feel to a larger concern. If you are not already organized in this way, it is liable to mean a major restructuring of your customer contact processes and organizations. Don't delay – without this change, nothing else can follow.

Agent's agenda

If you are an agent, you will have found a mix of material here, some of which is directly useful, and some of which will need management involvement to make it happen. Yours is a key position, and your input ought to be involved all along the way. Looking at an agenda for action consider how you can:

- improve the quality of your communication with your customers;
- make customers more likely to come back to your company;
- improve your written and verbal communication skills;
- ensure that customers' comments and suggestions are acted upon;
- know more about your own and your competitors' products and services;
- understand customers' problems and frustrations;
- give the glow to customers;
- know more about your customers, and think of them as real people;
- take charge of your own development;
- manage your stress.

Step by step

As a manager, you have more influence on the processes that support (or hinder) agents, and a wider view of what is happening. Your agenda should include:

- understanding customer processes;
- trying out customer processes and seeing what is irritating;
- ensuring that your site is easy to contact;
- looking into the use of natural language IVR, and minimizing traditional IVR menus;
- understanding the need to give customers a glow, and supporting agents in doing so;
- improving customer data availability to agents;
- examining recruiting and reward policies for agents to make sure you have the right quality of staff;
- looking at opportunities for training, both in customer care and supporting skills like time management and creativity;
- widening the agents' role to give more responsibility and empowerment;
- developing a climate of trust with agents;
- ensuring that technological developments are incorporated into the site;
- watching and learning from the competition;
- listening to your customers and your staff – and taking action.

Putting it into action

The two sections above provide templates for personal agendas. Pull out the key items that apply to you. Use the detail of this book to put some flesh on the items. Set yourself targets and timescales to get something done. When you're in a fast-paced business, you need clear goals and timescales.

The opportunity is there. You can vastly improve the service received by the invisible customer. Most of your competitors are unlikely to succeed in this as quickly as you will. Be prepared to make the difference – starting today.

Appendix 1

Further reading

This book is complete in itself, but it owes a huge debt to many other books and sources. Instead of providing a dry list of references, these short reviews should give a better feel for where you might go next to find out more on a particular topic. Many of these books are available from the Creativity Unleashed business bookshop at http://www.cul.co.uk/books.

General customer service

Bailey, K and Leland, K (1995) *Customer Service for Dummies*, IDG
One of the popular yellow 'For Dummies' books, taking a practical approach to customer service at the level of both specific tactics and putting together an overall improvement plan.

Clegg, B (2000) *Capturing Customers' Hearts,* Pearson Education
An insight into the special characteristics that make a company attractive to customers. Whether about a quirky product with character, a charismatic leader or a stunning approach to service, this book explores the wooing of the customer.

Peters, T and Austin, N (1985) *A Passion for Excellence,* Random House
Despite its age, this follow-up to *In Search of Excellence* still stands out as a picture of superior customer service driven by leadership.

Zemke, R and Woods, J A (1998) *Best Practices in Customer Service,* Amacom
The author of the 'Knock your socks off' service book teams up with quality-management specialist John Woods to pull together 35 articles about

great customer service. Rather systems- and organization-oriented, but doesn't forget the customer.

Call centres/Web

Bodin, M (1998) *Maximizing Call Center Performance,* Miller Freeman
This book takes you behind the scenes of some of the top call centres in North America to explore how they are using technology to serve their needs, and at the same time give good service to the customer. A good, case-study-driven view of call centres today.

Cusack, M (1998) *Online Customer Care – Strategies for Call Center Excellence*, ASQ
Cusack's book is a detailed view of call centre operations from a process viewpoint. With detailed diagrams of processes and options, it says a lot more about technology and systems than it does about customers, but what it does say is valuable.

Balanced scorecard

The balanced scorecard is a mechanism for getting a much better measure of performance than from a single axis of indication (such as cost saving). These books give a fuller picture of the balanced scorecard.

Bourne, M and Bourne, P (2000) *Understanding the Balanced Scorecard in a Week*, Headway
Not published at the time of going to press, but a shorter (cheaper) book than the others, one that could give a good summary of the practical use of the scorecard without the baggage.

Kaplan, R S and Norton, D P (1996) *The Balanced Scorecard: Translating Strategy into Action,* Harvard Business School Press
The definitive book in that it is by the inventors of the balanced scorecard, but received mixed reviews – after the impact of the original article, this seems to be a one-idea book, watered down with standard management theory to fill the 322 pages. Even so, worth considering.

Goran Olve, N, Roy, J and Wetter, M (1999) *Performance Drivers,* John Wiley & Sons
Subtitled 'A practical guide to using the balanced scorecard', this is an

attempt to go beyond the theory, including case studies from major organizations as well as practical advice. The authors are perhaps a trifle academic for a 'practical' book – but well worth considering.

Creativity

Creativity is an essential driver for making remote customer service work. Everything has to be that bit more effective to cope with the barrier between you and the customer. These books give some insights into getting more creativity into the company.

Birch, P and Clegg, B (2000) *Imagination Engineering*, Pitman Publishing
A very readable guide to being more creative in business, giving the reader a tool-kit for practical innovation.

Clegg, B (1999) *Creativity and Innovation for Managers*, Butterworth Heinemann
Less of a tool-kit on creativity and more a guide to getting started on an agenda for bringing creativity into the corporate culture.

Clegg, B (1999) *Instant Brainpower*, Kogan Page
A whole host of exercises to increase personal creativity. *Instant Brainpower* uses the popular 'Instant' format to provide techniques to improve creativity, memory and knowledge management in an instant.

Clegg, B and Birch, P (1998) *Instant Teamwork*, Kogan Page
With over 70 techniques to help teams be more creative, this is an excellent collection of exercises that can be undertaken in team meetings and training sessions, both to bring teams together and to help them work more effectively.

Clegg, B and Birch, P (1999) *Instant Creativity*, Kogan Page
If you need creativity but you haven't time for all the trappings, this could be the book for you. It is packed with over 70 techniques that can be used to generate creative ideas and solve problems in minutes.

Peters, T (1998) *The Circle of Innovation*, Coronet
The master of business cheerleading has excelled himself in this picture of how to achieve greatness for your company. Based on slides from his dynamic presentations, the layout of the book takes a little getting used to, but the approach to creativity in customer service is second to none.

Time management

Time management is essential if agents are going to give their best, and balance getting through enough contacts with really helping customers. These books give a guide to the ins and outs of time management.

Clegg, B (1998) *The Chameleon Manager*, Butterworth Heinemann
This book takes the concept of time management into the wider sphere of gaining the skills needed to thrive in the workplace of the new millennium. It identifies management of creativity, communication and knowledge as the key requirements, and includes a different perspective on time management.

Clegg, B (1999) *Instant Time Management*, Kogan Page
A real problem with time management is finding time to do it. This book of over 70 time management techniques allows readers to enhance their time management whenever they have a few minutes to spare without wasting precious time.

Hayes, M E (1996) *Make Every Minute Count*, Kogan Page
This book is in the quick-fire 'Better Management Skills' series, and is the only book in this section that is US-written – but the subject varies little between countries. Even more checklists and questionnaires than in Smith's book (see below). An excellent way of getting started in the subject.

Johns, T (1994) *Perfect Time Management*, Arrow
A handy pocket book giving an overview of time management practice from a very pragmatic viewpoint. Includes both background and detail (eg suggested forms for the agenda of a meeting).

Seiwert, L J (1989) *Managing Your Time*, Kogan Page
A very visual book with lots of diagrams, plans and cartoons – it'll either impress you (as it has apparently impressed more than 300,000 readers) or leave you cold. Particularly helpful if you like very specific guidance and information as juicy snippets.

Smith, J (1997) *How to be a Better... Time Manager*, Kogan Page
An Industrial Society-sponsored volume, Smith's book takes an easy-to-read, no-nonsense approach to time management. A fair number of checklists and short questionnaires to fill in along the way.

Stress management

Clegg, B (2000) *Instant Stress Management*, Kogan Page
Packed full of quick-to-use stress management techniques, this book is ideal for the high-pressure environments of call centres and Internet support centres, where there simply isn't time to read through a book.

Coscia, S (1998) *TeleStress – Relief for Call Center Stress*, Miller Freeman
A look at the specifics of stress in a call centre setting. Considers the causes of stress and looks at stress management techniques that are particularly valuable within call centres.

Fossum, L (1993) *Managing Anxiety*, Kogan Page
A quick guide to the nature of anxiety and how to conquer it. Fossum's book is short and has plenty of practical exercises to reduce this key component of stress.

Makin, P E and Lindley, P A (1991) *Positive Stress Management*, Kogan Page
Time management, good communication, relaxation and fitness come together to form the main parts of this practical guide to staying on top of work pressures. It also considers how we can stay in control and use others to manage stress.

O'Hanlon, B (1998) *Stress, The Commonsense Approach*, Newleaf
A good pocket book giving a general overview of stress and dealing with it. Gives rather a lot of space to alternative treatments and therapy, but otherwise well-balanced.

Towner, L (1998) *Managing Employee Stress*, Kogan Page
One of the 'Better Management Skills' series, aimed at giving a test-as-you-go run through stress in business. As the title suggests, concentrates solely on employees and takes something of an 'us and them' approach. Gives useful information on legislation.

Williams, S (1994) *Managing Pressure For Peak Peformance*, Kogan Page
The subtitle, 'The positive approach to stress', gives away the direction this interesting book takes. Rather than regarding stress as a necessary evil it concentrates on achieving a balance, reducing stress where appropriate, but making use of it to achieve in the workplace.

Other

Gall, J (1977) *Systemantics*, New York Times Book Company
A humorous guide to why systems work and particularly why they fail.
Gall's book labours the point occasionally, but it is still absolutely relevant
in providing an insight into the workings (and failings) of the sort of complex system that is central to providing support to the invisible customer.

Norman, D A (1988) *The Psychology of Everyday Things*, BasicBooks
Norman's book effortlessly illustrates how designers make us feel stupid by
rating appearance above usability when they design a product. When we
can't use an everyday object, we blame ourselves instead of the designer.
Essential reading if you want your site to be designed for customer friendliness. The updated version is called *The Design of Everyday Things*.

Semler, R (1994) *Maverick!*, Arrow
One of the best books ever written on the business benefits of trust. It's not
a textbook, but the biography of a company. Although the company was
located in Brazil during a time of runaway inflation and with potentially difficult unions, Semler took its disgruntled workforce and totally changed
their motivation by making trust a centrepiece of the way the company
operated.

Web sources

Web sites get out of date much faster than book references, but the following sites provided valuable resources on call centres, computer telephony
and customer service at the time of going to press:

Computer and Internet Telephony page – www.computertelephony.org
Computer Telephony site – www.telecomlibrary.com
The UK Call Centre Association – www.cca.org.uk
The UK Call Centre Management Association – www.ccma.org.uk
Call Center Management Review – www.servicelevel.com
The Incoming Calls Management Institute – www.incoming.com
Nortel Call Centre Academy – www.nortelnetworks.com/servsup/cca

Appendix 2

Natural language IVR ROI model

Introduction

The most significant technological change to impact on call centres at the start of the 21st century is natural language Interactive Voice Response (IVR). This technology does away with the unnatural nature of IVR where selection is by using the telephone keypad. It enables an automatic system to do significantly more of the work currently performed by human operators – meaning a major cost reduction – and is usable from any phone, including the old-fashioned rotary (pulse) phones.

This appendix contains the model of a spreadsheet developed by Unisys, one of the largest US computing and telecommunications firms: it is reproduced by kind permission of Unisys. The model was developed to show the return on investment (ROI) generated by a move to natural language IVR, and hence the payback period for the system. Unisys has built this model with the intention of selling its product, but it remains useful in its own right for getting a feel for the impact of natural language IVR on the call centre operation.

To make the workings of the spreadsheet clear, the example below has both sample data (column 2) and the actual typed input (column 3). Note that throughout, agents are referred to as 'Customer Service Representatives' (CSR), the term used by Unisys.

The model

Table A.1 Natural language IVR ROI model

	1	2	3
A	Annual call volume	1,200,000	1200000
B	Average handling time (total) in seconds	210	210
C	Per cent of calls handled by IVR	50%	50%
D	IVR per cent of average handling time	100%	100%
E	Per cent extra calls to be handled by NL Assistant	30%	30%
F	NL Assistant per cent of average handling time	85%	85%
G	Hourly base pay	$12.00	12.00
H	Fully loaded base pay	$20.40	G3*1.7
I	Average handling time (CSR) in seconds	180	180
J	Average calls/hour/CSR	16	3600/I3*0.8
K	Average CSR cost/call	$1.28	H3/J3
L	Average telephone service charge per minute	$0.12	0.12
M	Average telephone service charge per second	$0.002	L3/60
N	Per cent rotary usage	25%	25%
O	IVR seconds saved per call	40	40
P	IVR Annual savings	$48,000	O3*A3*C3*D3*M3
Q	Fully loaded headcount annual savings	$390,150	A3*E3*F3*K3
R	Total Annual savings – most probable case	$438,150	P3+Q3
S	Sensitivity – conservative annual savings (-25%)	$328, 612	0.75*R3
T	Sensitivity – optimistic annual savings (+25%)	$547,687	1.25*R3
U	Ports on system	72	72
V	Cost per port	$5,000	5000
W	System cost	$360,000	U3*V3
X	Most probably payback (months)	9.86	W3/(R3/12)
Y	Conservative payback (months)	13.15	W3/(S3/12)
Z	Optimistic payback (months)	7.89	W3/(T3/12)

Terms

A. **Annual call volume** – total number of calls received by the call centre or unit.
B. **Average handling time (total)** – average amount of time the caller is on the telephone dealing with either an IVR or customer service representative (CSR). This excludes ring time and time in queue (on hold). In high-volume call centres the average length of a customer service call ranges from two to four minutes. However in some areas, such as mortgages or technical assistance, calls can average six to ten minutes, or even more.
C. **Per cent of calls handled by IVR** – this is the percentage of the annual call volume that is handled by IVR before the introduction of the natural language system. In some banking applications this can be as high as 70 per cent. In many environments, some call types are fully handled by the IVR and some are partially handled by the IVR. To account for these different calls accurately, individual ROI spreadsheets should be done on each type.
D. **IVR per cent of average handling time** – the percentage of the average handling time spent dealing with the IVR. Where a call is fully handled by the IVR, this figure is 100 per cent. If a call is only partly handled by the IVR, for example when the IVR is collecting initial information before delivering the caller to a live agent, this is the percentage of total call time spent interacting with the IVR.
E. **Per cent extra calls to be handled by NL Assistant** – in this example, the natural language system will handle 60 per cent of the calls not being handled currently by the IVR (ie 30 per cent of the total call volume). This includes customers who haven't got touch-tone phones and new calls that don't fit with the existing IVR. It is assumed also that the natural language system will handle all calls currently handled by the IVR.
F. **NL Assistant per cent of average handling time** – Of the new IVR calls handled by the natural language system, some will leave the system to speak to a CSR. On aggregate the natural language system will cover this percentage of the handling time for these calls.
G. **Hourly base pay** – The average hourly pay for the CSRs handling the calls. This does not include benefit or overhead, but should factor in bonuses and commissions.
H. **Fully loaded base pay** – A loading factor is then added to the base pay to derive the full cost per hour. The default loading factor is 1.7, assuming 25 per cent on benefits, 35 per cent on facilities and training and

10 per cent on overtime. Companies with very high turnover rates will have an extra loading to add in. If the turnover cannot be dealt with, companies with 100 per cent turnover need to add in another 20 per cent to the loading, with lower rates of turnover factored accordingly. Turnover below 25 per cent can be ignored as it is covered by the facilities and training factor.

I. **Average handling time (CSR) in seconds** – average amount of time that a call is handled by a CSR. It is useful to have this information by call type, since aggregate statistics often hide substantial savings to be gained from automating some call types. These statistics are usually available from automatic call distributor (ACD) reports.

J. **Average calls/hour/CSR** – average number of calls a CSR handles in an hour, assuming 80 per cent of time spent on the phone.

K. **Average CSR cost/call** – hourly pay divided between the average calls handled.

L. **Average telephone service charge per minute** – this assumes that the caller is using a toll free (0800/800) number, and gives the average charge to the company of supporting that call. This will be used to provide the cost improvement on the conventional IVR calls.

M. **Average telephone service charge per second** – as L above, but for seconds.

N. **Per cent rotary usage** – percentage of customers who call in using rotary (pulse) phones rather than touch-tone. In 1999 this was around 25 per cent in North America, but in some countries is as high as 80 or 90 per cent of wired phones.

O. **IVR seconds saved per call** – the average difference between the call length using conventional IVR and the call length with a natural language system. This will vary significantly depending on the call type, but the 40-second figure used here is typical.

P. **IVR annual savings** – telephone charge savings based on using natural language rather than conventional IVR.

Q. **Fully loaded headcount annual savings** – cost of the CSR time which has been replaced by natural language IVR. As always with headcount savings, this needs to be carefully handled to make sure that savings are genuine rather than hypothetical.

The remainder of the entries give a 25-per-cent-either-way sensitivity analysis, and look at the payback time for purchasing a natural language system.

Index